The Library Association

LOOK UP – AND LEARN

Library Association adult independent
learning guidelines for libraries and
learning resource centres

Anthony L Bamber

LIBRARY ASSOCIATION PUBLISHING
LONDON

Published by
Library Association Publishing Ltd
7 Ridgmount Street
London WC1E 7AE

First published 1992

British Library Cataloguing in Publication Data:

Bamber, Anthony L
    Look up – and learn: Library Association adult independent
    learning guidelines for libraries and learning resource centres.
    I. Title
    025.5

    ISBN 1–85604–068–2

Typeset by the author.
Printed and made in Great Britain by Amber (Printwork) Ltd,
Harpenden, Herts.

Contents

Foreword

Four years after the publication of *Library services for adult continuing education and independent learning* by Raymond Fisher, the Library Association's Adult Learning and Libraries sub-committee is pleased to see the issue of this volume as a further tool for librarians and those working with them in the network of support for adult learners.

Much has happened since 1988 when the study by Vernon Smith, *Public libraries and independent learning*, provided the impetus for the first guide. Distinctions between independent learning, supported learning and formal tuition are even more difficult to make now. Learning technologies have been dramatically exploited for all three modes of learning and participation by adults continues to increase significantly. The challenge for librarians in all kinds of libraries to exploit their resources for learners has not been so great since the heady days in the late 18th and 19th century when libraries in academies, mechanics' institutes and the early public libraries were foremost learning resources.

This guide for the 1990s emphasises the learners and the librarians, not the type of library. It addresses the needs of learners for educational guidance and for a real choice of methods of learning. It explains the competences and knowledge required of librarians working within the support network.

The Adult Learning and Libraries sub-committee wishes to record its thanks to Tony Bamber for producing this guide within a tight timetable, and to all our colleagues in librarianship, education, publishing and broadcasting who gave their advice.

John Allred, *Chair*,
Library Association, Adult Learning and Libraries sub-committee

Preface

These guidelines owe their origin to the work of the Library Association's Adult Learning and Libraries Sub-Committee. It was this group that identified the need for a new set of official guidelines for a subject area that has been developing rapidly within libraries of all types. In many cases the developments have been encouraged both directly and indirectly by the work of the Employment Department and its Training, Enterprise and Education Directorate (TEED). The impetus is being encouraged to continue, as many of TEED's responsibilities devolve upon the Training and Enterprise Councils in England and Wales or the local enterprise companies in Scotland.

I have been grateful for the interest shown by all members of the Sub-Committee and for the support and assistance of John Allred (its chairman)and Alan Watkin who have watched over the project as it developed; at the same time Carl Clayton has represented the Library Association's interests with a pleasant and helpful efficiency.

Personally I hope that the book will allow librarians to choose appropriate levels of service to adult independent learners from within their own local resources in a way that will meet a growing need and give satisfaction to users and providers alike.

Tony Bamber
Dihewyd, Dyfed.

July 1992

1. The place of libraries in open learning

Learning – a lifetime experience

Libraries are the natural recourse for the formal and informal student, and for those seeking information or self-improvement. Libraries in recognized institutions of education – schools, colleges, polytechnics and universities are able to identify their clientele fairly clearly as those who attend the courses provided by that institution. In recent years the nature of this clientele has broadened to include wider age groups: for example, schools that admit adults to GCSE classes and colleges that seek to provide flexible learning courses for those in full-time employment. During the same period, central government has been encouraging the institutions to sell their education services to an ever-wider audience, and the competition of the market place has taken its place in the philosophy of academia.

Alongside these developments there continues to exist a wide and varied multitude of adult learners. They are also students in the wider sense of the term, in that they seek to widen and deepen the limits of their knowledge from a host of motives, ranging from a desire to explore further a personal interest to the imperatives of career development. A great many of these learners seek to advance their knowledge and abilities through constructive use of public library services; others enrol for distance learning courses such as those of the National Extension College, Open Tech or Open University while many seek to follow their interests through part-time classes at colleges, or with organizations such as the Workers' Educational Association and the University of the Third Age.

1

Guidelines

These guidelines seek to provide a framework for library service delivery to the adult independent learner. In preparing the guidelines it has been necessary to cater for libraries of all sizes and in very different environments; they include both the broad aspects of management strategy and detailed suggestions for day-to-day administration, being designed to serve as a base from which varying levels of service can be developed. The individual learner is the prime concern of these guidelines for service provision, whether this service be provided as part of a college-based distance learning course using open and flexible techniques, or through the resources of the public library service dealing directly with the needs of those learners who are outside the immediate orbit of the institutional world.

In this field three different terms are used to describe types of learning; these require some definition and understanding, especially as the scope of each can develop, overlap or interact with any of the others. They are: *distance learning,flexible learning* and *open learning:* all three approaches may be used by an individual described as an *adult independent learner.* None of these excludes any level of educational need, which may be for very basic skills, for developmental knowledge or for specific and detailed research study. It is also important to realize that the open learning approach is by no means relevant to every learning need.

Distance learning
Study undertaken away from formal classes, but within a defined study framework, often with tutor support.

Flexible learning
An organized study programme allowing students to progress at a speed of their own choosing.

Open learning
Learner-centred study, possibly in pursuit of a recognized qualification, usually using materials which have been prepared so that they may be used without tutor support and without barriers of time, previous qualifications or classroom attendance.

Independent learning
Study undertaken and controlled by an individual in her or his own way.

2

The learner

The adult independent learner is somebody who is studying on his or her own, often outside the formal education system. Purposive study in this way can often lead to progress into flexible and distance learning projects, or into a more formal course of college-based study.

Emphasis on the learner as an individual is deliberate and important. This emphasis is not new, indeed it is familiar to librarians in all types of library. It is, however, an emphasis that is easily and willingly acknowledged but less easily practised in the demanding world of cost-effectiveness. Independent learners are very individual; they do not fit into any recognized group and are now often seen as a college class of one alone, requiring a standard of service that may well be very extensive and which is certainly very personal. Above all, the service must be delivered in a broadly professional manner; the recipient needs to feel that her or his requirements are being met with understanding and in an unthreatening way. Where this is successful at the very first encounter with the library it will ensure that the learner continues to have trust in the efficiency and competence of the service thereafter.

The response

Libraries of all types are in a position to respond to the demands of adult independent learners. Libraries in seats of learning quite obviously have education as a priority objective, many in industry and commerce will be developing similar objectives as being relevant to the growing demand for workplace educational initiatives, or as an adjunct to the already accepted research and development function. Public libraries have traditionally accepted a broad-based education function alongside those of information, culture and recreation. These activities are dependent upon the combination of the availability of impartial advice, appropriate library stocks and of trained staff to exploit them, for the advantage of the individual.

Being in a position to respond to the impetus of adult independent learning does not automatically mean that a library will be willing to do so, but without such a willingness it is not possible to ensure that a real service is provided. At the same time the ramifications of a really in-depth service in this field can be considerable, ranging from initial educational guidance to the provision of effective tutor support. In another sense, libraries are frequently in the very best position to provide this type of service, simply as a result of their physical location within the community they serve – a situation particularly enjoyed by a majority of local public libraries. (A good example of the benefits to be derived from such a location can be found in the development of the Second Chance Centre in Rhyl, Clwyd, where the county council's education and library services joined forces, used the public library as a base and established an open learning centre that provided opportunities for adults to improve their basic skills using a variety of learning styles.)[1] In general, librarians have the ability to provide advice to the student through a service which is highly accessible, whether it be on a college campus, in a local adult education centre or on the high street. Librarians who staff these libraries are able to relate need to demand, to provide for their requirements from within their own extensive stocks, or to borrow through the highly developed local and national networks that exist to support some of the more individual demands made upon library services.

Each library needs to make its own assessment of the extent of both its current involvement with open and flexible learning provision and its desired depth of involvement, as materials become increasingly available and demand inevitably grows. Each library will need to adopt a structured approach to an agreed level of provision for the adult independent learner, which can then be marketed to users, advised to staff and developed in a progressive and purposive manner. These guidelines seek to allow such assessments and decisions to be made.

In the case of library services operating from more than one location, there is a need to make management decisions relating to the provision of open learning information and materials throughout the network, as well as the extent to which the requirements of independent learners can be met at any one location.

The seekers after information and knowledge will not always see themselves as students, even in the widest sense of the term; neither will they necessarily attach an education label to the subject of their quest. For example, a librarian encounters a plumber who always notices spelling mistakes in the local newspaper. He wonders how they happen and what is involved in proof-reading. The librarian

4

realizes that he does not want a college course to learn more about this interest, yet his willingness to learn certainly makes him a student of the principles and practice of proof-reading. Such an enquirer offers no clash with the demand for formal courses, does not require a wide range of learning materials, and does not add to demand for popular textbooks, but none the less he might be glad to meet an expert in the subject at some point. As a potential user of a library service the plumber could be easily scared away from this potential interest and personal development if there is any attempt, particularly at an early stage, to define the interest as educational, yet it is quite evidently such and places the enquirer firmly in the category of adult independent learner. If handled well at the outset there is every chance that, over a period, the plumber will progress to a greater understanding of his own abilities and to a more purposive use of both library and educational facilities.

Initial decisions

In many libraries the decision to provide open learning materials is likely to have been made as a result of the policy of the institution to which the library belongs. Thus colleges of further and higher education will already expect libraries and learning resource centres to hold multi-media learning materials, as will libraries associated with large commercial organizations where the value of open learning in personal staff development is now extremely well recognized and understood. In public libraries there may exist a more general commitment to the educational needs of the individual within the comprehensive nature of the requirements of the Public Libraries and Museums Act. But this commitment may not necessarily extend to an acceptance of the provision of open learning study packs, multi-media materials or access to educational guidance services. Where it does not exist it is important for the library authority to accept that the multi-media learning packs of the late twentieth century are very much the equivalent of the authoritative monographs of the previous century, which it was the function of public libraries to make available to those for whom the purchase of such introductions to learning was financially impossible.

Whatever the situation, the first decision has to be to accept or confirm responsibility for open learning library services in support of the adult independent learner. Subsequent decisions must then by made about what level of service to provide at each individual library within a library organization, what elements each should contain and what charges, if any, should be made. Performance measures must then be accepted for the defined level of service.

The minimum level of library service provided to the adult independent learner must be one of access and information. At this level the library staff will be trained to collect enquiries about learning opportunities, to provide basic information at the point of enquiry, to refer the enquirer to a study centre or careers service for access to educational guidance, where required, or to give an individual response direct to the enquirer. Libraries providing the minimum service will also need to function as a delivery and collection point for the materials and to maintain contact with the learners.

Libraries providing a more active level of service will have at least a basic collection of open learning materials with basic guidance available on site, together with access to the use of a personal computer. Full-scale library study centres will require a wide-ranging loan collection, on-site reference collection, computer, audio-visual equipment, specialist guidance staff and links with tutors and support networks. These levels of service are set out fully in Chapter 4.

Library first steps

For a library wishing to accept or confirm its involvement in open learning service provision the initial guideline steps are:
- make a commitment to education as a priority objective;
- decide to include open learning materials as part of the library stock;
- determine to provide a specifically individual service to each adult independent learner;
- map existing local provision and then identify the level of service to be provided, which may vary between individual library service points;
- ensure that the levels of service available are clear to the user and fully understood by staff;
- ensure that individual levels of service are found by the user to be professionally efficient and competent.

2. The learners

Independent and individual

A distinction must be made between the adult independent learner who has already been described as someone who is studying alone outside the formal education system and her or his counterpart, the full-time student undertaking a formal course of study within an educational institution. Vernon Smith, writing on behalf of the National Council for Educational Technology, has described such people as those 'who engage in specific learning activities on a regular or an occasional basis – either as individuals or in groups – without formally enrolling for a course with an education or training agency'.[2]

In addition to this, the individual can be often be identified more clearly through a prime characteristic of self-motivation and, very frequently, a secondary one of effective time management. These characteristics have been acknowledged by a number of initiatives undertaken by the Employment Department's Training, Enterprise and Education Directorate with an objective which is perhaps summarized in the phrase 'unlocking the potential of individual people by giving them the chance to acquire skills and qualifications'.[3] The directorate worked with companies to show how open learning could prove cost effective, improving both individual ability and company productivity;[4] it worked also with ten public library authorities, the Library Association and the British Association for Open Learning to show how the same results could be obtained by working directly with individuals, many of whom were either self-employed, or working for small companies.[5] These projects have shed a great deal of light on the variety of people for whom access to open learning has changed their lives and outlook. A similar set of achievements was recorded in the entries for an Independent Library Learner Award organized by Pergamon Open Learning in association with the Library Association as a contribution to the 1992 national Adult Learners Week. The following are a few examples from these various initiatives.

1 The **winner**, joined an adult basic education class in Bexley's Thamesmead Library, used the library computer and some of the Adult and Basic Skills Unit's learning materials to improve her writing skills and then used books to help her pass the driving test. She went on to gain the fork-lift truck operating licence. These achievements encouraged her to work for the City and Guilds certificate in communication skills and to study a foreign language with the BBC Ensemble learning pack.

2 The **family-run bakery** with 13 retail outlets which increased sales turnover by an average of 12 per cent in the 12 months following an open learning training programme and subsequently continued to record increases of sales above inflation afterwards.

3 The **driving instructor** who obtained his certificate after using Manchester Open Learning's Approved Driving Instruction Package, which he borrowed, together with other support material, from Flint Library in Clwyd. Having gained employment as a full-time driving instructor as a result, he graduated to managing the business in the owner's absence and hopes in due course to own his own driving school and become a driving examiner.

4 The **lighthouse keeper** facing redundancy who used open learning packs supplied by the Highland Regional Library Service to gain sufficient confidence to set up in business on his own.

5. The **medical technician** who, whilst caring for an invalid wife, progressed from adult basic education to GCSE and then A level human biology using a home study programme from Sudbury library in Suffolk.

Altogether, the work undertaken so far shows a wide variety of situations in which open learning can be of benefit to individual people and to firms. The extent to which it is necessary to involve formal college tuition will vary. Many colleges have already realized this and are active in the preparation of open learning resource packs which may be used either entirely without tutor support or with a minimum amount on a distance learning basis. In general it is now viewed as a developing market. This could mean that, on some occasions at least, librarians will need to remember that their prime responsibility is to the user, rather than to an institution, when recommending the best approach to a would-be learner.

Likely groups of learners

Although all independent learners are characterized by their individuality, it is possible to identify some broad groups into which many of them fall.

Self-employed business people and those responsible for running a business employing two or three people, constitute a primary target group as far as economic development is concerned. The growth in each of these areas of economic activity has been high in recent years and the training needs of both these groups are hard to meet on a formal basis. Chambers of Commerce and Training and Enterprise Councils each have interests in ensuring that the small business enterprise can remain efficient, effective and up-to-date, not least in the developing opportunities of the Single European Market.

Women returners are people often targeted by employers of all sorts; they constitute a group that is often seen as a source of part-time (and perhaps relatively cheap?) labour. Within this group are a great many individuals with latent skills and abilities; they may have only limited time to improve or update these skills, yet by so doing they are bound to improve their chances to obtain worthwhile employment, and may also, in the process, find an increase in their self-esteem.

People who need a 'second chance' educationally form a larger group than might be expected.[6] Indeed, there were 57,000 enquiries to the BBC helpline operated for two weeks in 1992 within a specific *Second Chance* initiative. They have needs that range from the very basic ability to read or to count and add up, on to the ability to write grammatical English or to speak it effectively. The ability to read and write in the Welsh language can also be a basic skill requirement of adults who live in Wales but are only able to speak their native language.[7] Allied to this category are those for whom English is a second language. The Second Chance group also includes many who left school as early as possible, who may well have a mastery of basic skills, but who have never really fulfilled their full learning potential. The Open University has pioneered distance learning for this group. It is now supplemented by the Open Polytechnic, the Open College and the Open College of the Arts. Students registered with all these bodies require access to information and supplementary reading, although the increase in demand may cause some concern where these institutions make limited funding provision to meet it. Despite all these opportunities there are still very many people with some educational attainment who wish to enhance their qualifications but for whom the formal educational world remains off-putting.

Would-be learners in older age groups sometimes lack the confidence to embark upon a course, perhaps because they have no formal qualifications at all, or else because their active educational days seem so long ago. Library services are well placed to help folk in this category.

The same is true of potential learners who are physically isolated from formal educational sources, such as the lighthouse keeper referred to earlier. There are many parts of the country, and not necessarily very remote ones, where inadequate public transport inhibits attendance at classes, or where distances are simply too great. In most of these cases library services are still available through small service points or mobile libraries.

Another group of adult independent learners comprises those for whom the college courses have proved inadequate, perhaps because the class has been full or under-subscribed; some people may even be too constrained by time (day of week, pace of learning or starting at a difficult time of the year). In each of these cases open learning can prove the right answer.

For the retired, open learning can prove a doorway to fascination. Here the constraints of career and the demands of home and family have in many cases dropped away, leaving an opening which can be filled by courses of all sorts, to the great satisfaction of all concerned.

Finally, a group which may well be composed of many from any of the groups mentioned above. These are people for whom the advantages of the more formal course need to be proved. This can often be done by using an open learning course as a foretaste of the learning experience and as a completely confidential and personal assessment of learning ability. This group can benefit greatly from all that a library has to offer and can also become a recruitment source for college courses, if handled sympathetically.

By taking care to note the specific needs of the individuals concerned, as well as other relevant social factors, it is possible to evaluate the type and amount of library support judged to be necessary. Many of these factors can well be elicited during the guidance process dealt with in Chapter 2, but the process has to be dealt with tactfully, especially at first, lest the first tentative enquiry be stifled before initial confidence in the library and its abilities has had a chance to become established. The process is very much a part of ascertaining the library needs of the learner so that the librarian may provide the most useful and relevant help, in such a way that the learner can appreciate its purpose.

Although this process may well involve the librarian making some form of record about the learner, at no time should there be any suggestion that data about an individual is being collected for some bureaucratic purpose. When such a record is kept it is best done manually and not as part of any computerized system, and the data should be restricted to objective and factual information. The learner should always be aware of the record and of its contents; when the need for it has passed then it should be destroyed. The following elements of information will be useful.

Educational background and learning experience

All adults have a record of learning experience, even if they do not immediately see it as such. Examples of common achievements are

11

learning to swim, riding a bicycle or driving a car. Many parents bring up children without having much formal tuition, yet they certainly undergo a learning experience in the process, as indeed does the child! The good news for embryonic adult learners is that they are not starting from ground zero and already have a solid foundation upon which to build; they also have the first course of building blocks: their self-motivation.

School and study experiences will vary considerably, with many people being anxious to overcome the problems of a poor educational background. Ability to hold a conversation, to write or to count and add up are often taken for granted by library staff, yet the lack of these very basic skills is often the reason behind a potential adult learning enquiry. The normal helpful and understanding approach of library staff can play a large part in beginning the process of overcoming the learner's embarrassment at this perceived failure, while the positive examples of proven ability can start to establish a good learner/library relationship.

The seeker after basic education is unlikely to have an understanding of the way in which a library may be used to assist the learning process, but many others at different levels of educational attainment may be equally unable to make the most of the facilities which a modern library service can offer. It will always prove helpful, both to the learner and to the librarian, to establish how much is known about library services at an early stage in the relationship.

Many adult learners are seeking to build upon previous educational experiences; in these situations it is helpful to have an understanding of the base line from which further learning will begin, and a note of levels of education and specific academic achievements should be made. Evaluation of the level of achievement against that required in the course of study the learner has in prospect can sometimes reveal a mismatch of the two. This should not mean that the learner needs to be discouraged, simply that his or her intentions should be understood at the outset by both learner and librarian, or that the possibilities for educational guidance be noted or pursued.

Motivation

Some indication of motivations may well emerge from the information collected about educational background, but generally these are as varied as the learners themselves. Self-improvement is often a very powerful motivator; it is frequently linked to career development, especially in an environment where emphasis on training and qualifications is growing. It may also relate to the acquisition of specific knowledge to help develop a small business. In this context it is interesting to note that there has been strong growth in both managerial and professional employment and in self employment during the second half of the 1980s.[8]

On the other hand, the learner may well be fulfilling a long- held interest, developing a hobby or relaxing in learning for its own sake, perhaps in conjunction with the Open University or the University of the Third Age. It certainly helps the librarian to know whether the learner is working with a group, or is studying entirely alone.

Level of study

Learners' needs range from the very basic to the very advanced. By establishing the level of study need the librarian will be able to evaluate the level of material to be provided. Although this may sound very obvious, it is often necessary to ensure that the learner's perception of elementary or advanced studies coincides with that normally understood in the educational world.

Personal situation

Every individual learner will be undertaking the course of study in the face of a number of difficulties. It helps to understand the personal situation on each occasion. Single parenthood, family demands, physical disabilities, lack of study space at home, physical restraints such as hospital or prison, awkward working hours, or the supposed leisure of retirement can all be very relevant to the learner's progress.

Course of study

The course of study is the object of the exercise, yet only after putting the learner into context as a person is it possible to give proper consideration to the learning involved. In an ideal world the course would be constructed on a purely individual basis as a result of a thorough in-depth guidance programme undertaken with the student. In practice, of course, this is very unlikely to happen. Rather, the learner will need to go away from the first encounter with something positive to do on the basis of mutually perceived study needs. The librarian will need to identify:

- the specific subject to be studied;
- the hoped-for level of attainment;
- the current level of study skills;
- the initial level of study;
- the current level of information skills;
- the most appropriate study media;
- guidance needs;
- current or potential links with educational institutions.

Study skills

The great strength of the adult independent learner is his or her motivation, yet although keenness alone may well seem enough, the learner will be helped considerably if it is channelled and directed in the most effective way. For many, the decision to enter upon a course of study has been made as a result of a personal realization that this is necessary in order to achieve a personal goal or ambition, hence the high level of motivation. It does not follow automatically that the would-be learner possesses the knowledge needed to put the decision into practice.

After the initial decision has been made, the learner needs to come to an understanding of his or her own position on the educational ladder. In a well ordered world this decision would be the outcome of the guidance process outlined in Chapter 3, but in practice the learner will need some encouragement to get that far along the road. Before reaching this point many learners need to test the reality of the decision to undertake study at all. Here the librarian will normally be able to make an initial evaluation that can contribute to the building of confidence that encourages the embryonic learner towards successful study.

The very first study skill required is invariably already present: motivation. This commitment needs to be encouraged by the setting of realistic learning targets, together with some mechanism to review these regularly, revising them if necessary to ensure that progress keeps pace with ability and thus maintains the initial impetus and motivation. The librarian can be an effective sounding board for the learner undertaking this process, while the maintenance of such contact may well enable the learner to be directed towards more detailed guidance and more advanced courses as time goes on.

Many of the other skills required for effective study can be developed with the aid of books from the library stock. The follow-on requirement from target-setting is that of timetabling, which in turn will include, later on, time for and methods of revision.

Within the overall timetable some attention will need to be given to the primary study skills of:

- reading;
- taking and organizing notes;
- memorizing;
- interpretation of text and diagrams;
- writing.

At some later stage the learner may also need to devote specific attention to the techniques involved in facing up to and taking examinations.

Any library should be able to respond to these needs by making available some time to understand the learner's actual level of ability and by providing books to help the learner develop these study skills. The library should also act as a point of contact to give the learner access to personal tuition in any of these basic skills, should that be required.

Information skills

Many learners will have no previous experience of using libraries for purposive reading and study and it is by no means uncommon for many people to feel intimidated at the prospect. This is likely to be particularly true in the case of the larger public and academic libraries.

An initial appreciation of the learner's situation will have been made as part of the first assessment of the enquirer's needs. This will often reveal uncertainty or hesitation about the function and use of library services. For the good of the enquirer, and indeed for the good of the library, this need should be addressed as soon as possible; certainly the student must be put at ease and be made aware that it is the librarian's pleasure to reveal these mysteries.

Each student's need for information skills becomes apparent during the exploration of study skills, as she or he is encouraged to identify specific study needs. The topics to be studied and the level at which the study is to take place need to be clearly understood before the information can be sought. From that point the student can be helped to understand the nature of information sources and their organization.

Adult independent learners may well welcome a course in the development and use of information skills: indeed, many libraries organize these, usually making a charge to enrol. Topics to be covered should include:

- defining information needs;
- sources of information;
- organization of information sources;
- library catalogues;
- library shelf arrangements;
- use of bibliographies;
- using books: contents lists, indexes, standing of author and publisher, currency of information;
- periodicals and abstract journals;
- computerized information retrieval; keywords and search techniques;
- inter-library loans;
- copyright and photocopying.

It is unlikely that all of these will be relevant immediately, therefore the student must be made aware above everything else that librarians are there to be **asked** for information.

Finance for learning

The ability of an adult independent learner to finance his or her course of study will obviously vary enormously between individuals. This section looks at the various situations in which learners can find themselves and the choices which may be necessary as a result.

The cost of open learning packs ranges from £10 to over £2000; many of them are bound to be outside the resources of a lot of people. College courses also have price tags, some of which can be met by grants from local education authorities or from employers. Even where grants are available there may be other factors, such as child-minding, which still make the cost too high, although open learning then becomes an alternative to be considered.

Funding initiatives seem to be related more to career development than to overcoming unemployment. The learning opportunities being promoted through some of the larger industrial firms and by Training and Enterprise Councils in England and Wales, and Local Enterprise Companies in Scotland, are growing in significance and range.[9] For employees covered by company-funded arrangements, many of which may well be operated in conjunction with local colleges, or be using open learning techniques, there is every reason to use the opportunity to its fullest extent. Learners following courses funded in this way will be encouraged to make use of library facilities within colleges and large firms. Librarians will need to work with local networks in order to ensure that the right facilities are made available and that individuals obtain all the relevant support. In other cases librarians and the educational guidance networks are able to refer learners towards details of welfare support; here the differences in cost between full-time and part-time study must also be taken into account.

Public library provision of open learning materials has been dependent upon local library authority policies. The statutory responsibility of a public library service to provide a comprehensive library service has been seen to apply solely to books, although many authorities have moved further into multi-media provision, albeit without being under the same legal obligations. As a result the adult independent learner has to check local policy before being in a position to assess the likelihood of borrowing a range of open learning materials as freely as books. Following on from the successful pilot projects undertaken in ten public library authorities, the Employment Department is moving towards grant-aiding the much wider availability of multi-media learning resources through public libraries.[10] This should prove particularly beneficial to people emp-

17

loyed in small business units, as well as to the unemployed. There is no certainty that access to these materials will always remain free, as it is for books, but there is good reason to hope that it will usually be so, since the purpose of the exercise is exactly the same as the very long-standing education function of the public library service.

3. Information and educational guidance

Guidance in perspective

The differences between the functions of making information available and of providing specific advice and educational guidance have usually been quite clear to librarians and library staff; however, such distinctions tend to be much less clear to both educationalists and students. The adult independent learner will not easily be able to differentiate between the two, nor should this be necessary. Librarians, however, will need to address the provision of information in two parts: that which relates to information about education, training and learning opportunities; and that which relates to active use of the library, its stock and systems. This chapter deals with each in turn, concentrating initially on the educational guidance aspect.

The Unit for the Development of Adult Continuing Education's National Education Guidance Initiative (UDACE and NEGI) has researched this field quite extensively. In 1986 *The challenge of change* was published by UDACE (since amalgamated with the Further Education Unit). It included a seven-part definition of the activities of educational guidance work, only one of which is the provision of information. The definition as a whole provides an important base from which to help the would-be student, and for our purposes that description includes the adult independent learner. The seven parts of the definition are: informing, advising, counselling, assessing, enabling, advocating and feeding back. UDACE says:

> In practice the seven activities are closely interrelated.
> Thus, for example, the choice of what information to pre-
> sent to a client, and how to do so, itself involves an 'assess-
> ment' of that client, whether or not this is consciously done.
> In the same way, the confidence building role of the
> 'enabler' often depends upon counselling skills. Without
> an adequate base of information none of the activities are
> [sic] possible, but a service which seeks only to provide
> information cannot, in any adequate way, meet the guid-
> ance needs of its clients.[11]

For librarians in most academic libraries the perceived barrier
between information and advice has already been removed as far as
educational guidance is concerned, and the same is often true of
those librarians practising in large industrial organizations where
open learning programmes have been introduced as part of purposive staff development. However, in many public libraries the distinction is still deeply felt and will need to be addressed before a
really effective service can be provided in this field. The fundamen-
tal ingredient for success has to be through partnership with the
education and guidance specialists.

Work designed to evaluate the potential for open learning delivery through public libraries, which was undertaken by ten public
library authorities on behalf of the Employment Department,
obtained useful information on the need to provide educational
guidance. The project, which took place between August 1989 and
March 1990, is detailed in the Library Association evaluation report
by John Allred and Peggy Heeks. Libraries involved in the project
established open learning services for unsponsored individuals on a
public access basis and showed such provision to be very worthwhile. The nature of the project was such that the timescale for evaluation was too short to establish how far along the road of advice
and counselling it would be necessary for public librarians to go. On
the other hand, it did indicate that many of the users felt able to discuss their learning needs with library staff and found these discus-
sions, with their impartial approach, helpful.

Many of the open learning packs in this project were used without tutor support, and thus the learners involved were often those

on the first stage of an educational ladder. Some would neither need nor wish to climb any of the subsequent available rungs, but as the projects developed to meet the objective of achieving in public libraries 'a level of operation that supports continuation of the service beyond Department of Employment funding', the needs for more responses – and probably in greater detail – to enquiries and to requests for educational guidance were set to grow. As part of this growth it became evident that the public library service could be an excellent recruiting ground through which suitable students could enrol on college courses. Consequently active co-operation between colleges and public libraries was found to be of benefit to both, as well as to the learners themselves.[12]

The activities of educational guidance

With the above possibilities in mind, each of the seven activities which comprise full educational guidance is now examined.

Informing

UDACE defines the informing function as:

> Providing information about learning opportunities and related support facilities available, without any discussion of the relative merits of options for particular clients. Since most published educational information is produced for promotional purposes 'pure' information is rare.[13]

Information in this context is seen as relating entirely to courses available in the public, voluntary and commercial sectors of education and training. The related stage of the active identification of library stock to meet a learning need is consequently a function within each of the subsequent stages of advising, counselling and assessing.

Information about learning opportunities is provided from leaflets and brochures produced by local education authorities, colleges, universities, voluntary and commercial organizations, and from computer databases on education and training opportunities (of which more than 200 have been identified in the United Kingdom).[14] Library systems seeking to provide effective access to this type of information need to:

- produce their own literature about adult learning opportunities within the library;
- maintain comprehensive, up-to-date and well displayed giveaway collections of leaflets and brochures for the agreed catchment area;
- keep a reference collection of all giveaway literature, plus copies of up-to-date detailed prospectuses;
- provide a publicly available subject index to the reference collection;
- promote the value of the literature service with the literature providers to ensure that they understand the consequences of non-provision;
- be a Training Access Point (TAP);
- have access to appropriate databases of learning opportunities;
- ensure that staff trained in the use of these information sources are available to work with enquirers.

Advising

This is the stage at which the learner is encouraged to relate the basic information provided at the initial enquiry to his or her own needs. The UDACE definition refers to:

> helping clients to interpret information and choose the most appropriate option. To benefit from advice clients must already have a fairly clear idea of what their needs are.[15]

To many librarians the process of helping people to clarify their needs in order to provide the information required is part and parcel of everyday activity, and work with adult independent learners is no exception to this. Consequently the UDACE seven-part approach to educational guidance that separates out this helping process from the counselling and assessing functions helps to clarify the number of different activities which are normally wrapped together within the librarian's view of information.

In order to undertake the advisory role in this context libraries can reasonably provide staff:

- at a clearly defined point of enquiry;
- with the ability to provide **impartial** guidance;
- who themselves understand the information being offered to clients;
- who can help the client relate that information to expressed learning needs;
- with the ability to identify clients who are uncertain of their needs;
- who have the knowledge of referral procedures giving access to counselling and assessment services for clients who need help to identify their specific learning requirements.

Within a library there is another dimension which is part of the advising process. When appropriate this requires library staff to:

- link the learning need with items of library stock in the first instance, and not necessarily with a college course. (The stocking of open learning materials is a major boost to the effectiveness of this process.)
- help learners to use library stock, catalogues, bibliographies and other facilities effectively;
- guide learners in planning their learning activities and in setting their objectives;
- provide book lists where necessary, which should be annotated if possible.

Counselling

Librarians generally do not regard counselling as part of their area of responsibility, although helping people to find access to sources of counselling comes within the remit of information provision. However, within the field of educational guidance the distinction is not quite so cut and dried.

Again, the UDACE definition is a helpful place to start. This aspect of the seven part guidance function is described as:

> working with clients to help them to discover, clarify, assess and understand their learning needs and the various ways of meeting them. Clients requiring counselling are likely to be unclear about their needs and require time to explore their feelings about the options, and counselling is therefore more likely to involve a series of contacts with a single client.[16]

Potential adult independent learners who bring their enquiry to a library frequently do so because the library is impartial, non-threatening and in the broad business of education. This is the reason why so many libraries have become actively involved with adult basic education, with librarians frequently becoming tutors for such programmes. At other levels, too, the same principle applies. These may encompass the intending tourist who wants to learn at least something of a foreign language, or the small businessman who needs to learn more about finance and balance sheets. In each of these instances the librarian will recognize that the enquiries just described are unlikely to be expressed in this way by the enquirers. 'Where can I get a course on Portuguese?' might be the question posed by a potential A-level student, a landlady trying to understand a visitor, or the intending tourist; in any event the librarian will undertake some of the elements described here as counselling in order to help the enquirer to identify his or her precise learning needs.

On other occasions the level of counselling required will be far deeper; educational guidance is not easily separated from vocational guidance, and the need for an assessment of individual potential begins to impinge more heavily upon the counselling process; for this, more specialized abilities are required and the librarian will need to refer learners to the right agency in appropriate cases. It is here that active links with local educational establishments and networks become of particular importance, with the work of education tutors and/or guidance workers being able to complement the information role of the librarian.

For the librarian it is at the counselling stage that the importance of proper training really needs to be emphasized. The purpose of such training is to ensure that the librarian is able to relate to the needs of the client in an impartial manner and that the client is able to appreciate the implications of her or his study need and also able to receive and understand accurate information about advice agencies and the availability of grants.

Assessing

Although the assessment of learning ability appears to follow on from counselling within the educational guidance structure it is in fact difficult to separate the two quite so clearly in practice, as is evident from the UDACE definition of assessing as:

> helping clients, by formal or informal means, to obtain an adequate understanding of their personal, educational and vocational development, in order to enable them to make sound judgements about the appropriateness of particular learning opportunities.[17]

The librarian's response to an enquiry for information on any subject will involve some assessment of the level of ability of the user, so that the material offered in response to the request is appropriate to both subject and individual. It is often the nature of library involvement with adult independent learners to find that they are exactly that – independent. Any initial concerted effort to direct an enquirer into a formal method of assessment may well result in entirely losing that person's interest. But here again, the librarian's approach has the advantage since it centres upon an obligation to the individual as an individual client whose needs are all-important.[18] This person-centred approach frequently means that a trusting relationship can be established between an adult independent learner and the library on an informal basis. As a result the suggestion that the time has come for a move to a formal method of assessment can well be made at the right time in the learner's educational progress, or encouragement can be given to the learner's own developing personal awareness and self-development.

Librarians are equipped to assess information skills and, to an initial extent at least, the level and currency of the study skills of would-be independent learners. Both these skills frequently have to

25

be learnt or relearnt, particularly if the learner left school with few academic qualifications at the earliest possible age and has had little or no experience of education since then. These concerns are dealt with in Chapters 5 and 6.

Enabling

When the time comes for the adult independent learner to make her or his own decision to seek involvement with educational institutions (and this may as well be on the very first visit to a library as on the umpteenth) then the fifth of UDACE's principles comes into play. The enabling role is described as:

> supporting the client in dealing with the agencies providing education or training, or in meeting the demands of particular courses. This may involve simple advice on completing application forms, advice on ways of negotiating changes in course content or arrangements, or assistance to independent learners. A further kind of enabling is provided through 'Access' and 'Wider Opportunities' courses which may offer both group guidance and the teaching of study skills.[19]

As with the need for assessment, the enabling role can be best performed by the librarian within an effective local network of education guidance. If this network does not already exist, establishing it may provide the opportunity to build up mutual trust and support. The provision of the simple advice suggested is likely to be straightforward for most librarians, but the ways of negotiating educational obstacles will require different skills and the support of the education specialist. Assistance to the independent learner is very much within the capability of the librarian in the first instance, while the value and importance of the local support network (and the librarian's role within it) is covered in detail in Chapter 4.

Advocating

Advocacy is not regarded as one of the librarian's professional skills, neither is it likely to be a requirement for a librarian outside the local networks in the field of educational guidance. To put this aspect of

26

the work into context it is useful again to quote the UDACE definition of this function, which is seen as:

> negotiating directly with institutions or agencies on behalf
> of individuals or groups for whom there may be additional
> barriers to access or to learning (e.g. negotiating excep-
> tional entry arrangements or modifications to courses).[20]

The thrust of this definition is towards the formal and institutional educational world, but librarians should not immediately dismiss
the function as a result. The need for advocacy may well arise during the course of the counselling aspect of guidance and may well
require the librarian in an academic library at least to initiate some
action on behalf of the student, albeit with an appropriate specialist.
On other occasions, the needs and/or expectations of the adult independent learner may well not be met simply because what the
library can provide is not sufficient. In such circumstances the
librarian to whom the learner has come for assistance may well need
to become an advocate with more senior managers for improved
stock or services on behalf of the individual whose voice may not
otherwise be heard.

In the library environment this aspect of educational guidance
must not be overlooked, although it is unlikely to take up a large
proportion of staff time. However, a management acceptance of the
need to include the advocating function within guidance training
and delivery (and an understanding of what this means in terms of
management response) is important.

Feeding back

Feedback is an aspect of information work with which librarians are
very familiar. In the context of open learning and the adult independent learner it is a particularly important part of overall service
delivery. In general, feedback works in two directions, both to the
provider and to the user, with the librarian in the familiar, but not
necessarily comfortable, role of the intermediary. The UDACE definition of feeding back does not see the function quite so widely:

> gathering and collating information on unmet, or inap-
> propriately met, needs and encouraging providers of learn-
> ing opportunities to respond by developing their provision.

27

This may involve practical changes (e.g. changing the presentation of course information or changing timetables) or curricular ones (e.g. designing new courses for new client groups, or changing the way in which existing courses are taught to make them more appropriate for adult learners).[21]

Undoubtedly all these aspects of feeding back may be undertaken by the librarian, who will need, in many instances, to pass on the comments to others better placed to initiate action. Librarians are certainly well placed to give feedback to providers about ways in which they might improve their presentation of information, for example, by suggesting refinements to leaflets and brochures either from their own experience or prompted by learners' responses. On other occasions the feedback may well be about course material and presentation, with the librarian able to operate in an objective, yet neutral role. In such circumstances there remains the responsibility to ensure that answers are forthcoming and passed back to the student who originated the query. As a public relations exercise this really is quite vital, although not easy to ensure. The way in which large organizations frequently fail to respond to individual problems is well known. Usually this is because these problems are not priorities for the person who should provide an answer and for whom there is no imperative of face-to-face contact to provide motivation.

Within the library itself the gathering of information on unmet, or inadequately met, needs may well be a most appropriate task because it is likely, in the first instance, to reflect upon the stock of the library, or upon the ability of the library to obtain the appropriate stock to meet the learner's need. Here the requirements of feedback may necessitate an explanation to the student of the reasons why such stock is not available, and the advocacy function may have to be exercised on behalf of the library service so that the learner can gain an appreciation of the problems which have led to his disappointment.

Library information

In addition to the needs of the independent learner for guidance and support there will also be needs for information about materials and facilities. These must be taken in conjunction with the agreed levels of library service approved for an individual library or for a library system as a whole.

Information about materials will include open learning packages, supporting workbooks, books and periodicals, reference and audio-visual materials, computer software, radio and television pro-grammes and their linked learning materials, as well as recorded programmes available for use in the library. These matters are dealt with in detail in Chapter 5.

Information about facilities will include access to equipment such as personal computers, photocopiers, video and cassette players, meeting and study space and the availability of educational and library guidance. Aspects of library guidance have been covered ear-lier and the other aspects of access to learning facilities are dealt with in Chapter 4.

Much of this chapter has followed the structure of the UDACE seven-part definition of educational guidance and has shown that librarians can make very effective contributions to the whole guid-ance process. It would, however, be a mistake to assume that this role can be adopted in isolation. The need for considerable training has to be accepted, as has the need to work as closely as possible with the local educational guidance service for adults; above all, libraries must seek to undertake library work with adult indepen-dent learners at a high level of effectiveness (including aspects of educational guidance) whilst developing close understandings of the ways in which the education specialists help and serve learners as well. Public librarians are well advised to read the report of the 1989/90 survey undertaken by the National Educational Guidance Initiative and the Library Association by Carole Barnes and John Allred,[22] while librarians in all types of library will find much useful information in Linda Butler's *Case studies in educational guidance for adults* [23] and in NEGI's handbook *Delivering educational guidance for adults*.

4. Access and facilities

The advantages of libraries

Libraries generally have a number of features which make them ideal places for the adult independent learner and upon which library managers can build in developing open learning services. The most important of these are given below.

Community location

Libraries always seek to be at a focal point within the community they serve, whether this be on a university or college campus, in the local high street or in a city centre. In most cases buildings have been designed to serve that community and to belong within it; they are familiar and have a record of personal service, impartiality and independence. Library buildings are very visible and accessible.

Availability

Library hours of opening are arranged, as far as possible, to allow use of the service at times convenient to the majority of people within the community it is designed to serve. Libraries serving industrial or commercial enterprises will normally be available during core working hours at least, while college libraries have recommended standards designed to provide a service at times convenient to the majority of students and staff alike, including opening in the evening. Similarly public libraries are normally available on some evenings each week (at least until 7, if not 8pm) and also on Saturdays, thus helping learners who are at work, or otherwise constrained in the times they are able to visit the library.

Study orientated

The image of the library as a quiet place is well known. In academic libraries this is an established feature and in public libraries it is preserved in reference libraries, study areas and homework rooms. Schools encourage young people to use both their own and public libraries for study purposes. Libraries provide space for reading, writing and thinking; frequently for listening, viewing, word processing and personal computing as well. Alongside the provision of study space there is the benefit of access to a wide-ranging library stock including reference books. In larger libraries there will be access to information databases both on-line and on CD-Rom, and to wider ranges of study materials.

Trained and qualified staff

Library staff are trained to provide access to information, to arrange information sources in a logical fashion and to make them available to their clients. As intermediaries, librarians and their staffs, with their knowledge of information sources and points of referral, are able to save the adult independent learner hours of searching. They have easy access to the facilities of the British Library and inter-library loan services, which seem always to surprise both regular and new users alike when books are borrowed from many different parts of the country.

Local support networks

All libraries have established links within their own communities; library systems have wider links which often stretch farther afield or, through their senior staff, with related institutions, their policy makers and managers. In many areas there has grown up a tradition of adult education providers, local education authorities, colleges and public libraries, working to co-ordinate activities at a policy level, supplemented by day-to-day contacts between practitioners working directly with clients. These networks can provide the basis for support to the adult independent learner who taps into it automatically, and probably unwittingly, as part of the service.

Levels of service

The availability of open learning materials does not have to be on the basis of a comprehensive approach at every level of library service. Within a library system there needs to be a policy decision about the level of service to be provided at each service point, while individually managed libraries will need to make the same decision solely for themselves. It is suggested that the level of service to be provided at each library should be selected in principle from one of the following, each of which is amplified in Chapter 5 :

Level 1. Contact point (passive)

The primary functions of the service for the adult independent learner at this level would be to:

- act as an information point about learning opportunities;
- be a reception and referral point for open learning enquiries;
- act as a delivery and collection point for the loan and return of open learning materials.

Libraries operating at this level are likely to be the smaller public library service points, secondary or outlier libraries within large firms and research establishments and some libraries on the smaller campus within a distributed college or educational institution, probably open for fewer than 30 hours per week.

Level 2. Delivery centre (active)

The library acting as a delivery centre for independent learning and open learning materials would be committed to:

- service level one responsibilities;
- stocking a basic collection of open learning materials;
- providing flexible loan arrangements suited to the needs of the adult independent learner and related to the nature of the course material being borrowed;
- making study facilities available, including use of a microcomputer;
- selling copies of workbooks associated with open learning courses;
- responding to adult learning enquiries using staff trained for this purpose;
- providing a basic level of adult educational guidance on site;
- offering access to in-depth educational guidance at an associated location within a reasonable distance for the learner.

In general, libraries in this category would be open at least 30 hours per week and would be a regular community focus, such as the main library in a small college, an average industrial library, or the public library serving a medium-sized town or a suburban area in a large city.

Level 3. Study centre (full service)

Libraries in this category are fully committed to the provision of open learning services and to assisting the adult independent learner through the on-site availability of:

- service level two responsibilities;
- a wide-ranging loan collection of open learning materials;
- maintenance of reference and giveaway literature collections;
- workbooks and related materials available for sale;
- designated staff trained to provide a full range of educational guidance;
- full access to local networks able to provide vocational guidance, training opportunities and tutorial support;

- study facilities comprising:
    space to read and write;
    playback equipment for working with video and
    audio tapes;
    microcomputer access for interactive video and
    other learning programs;
- access to tutors for consultation in conjunction with
    open learning courses and for the marking of course
    assignments. A charge might be made for these services.

Libraries willing and able to offer an open learning service at this
level will obviously require considerable commitment at all levels.
They will certainly be major libraries within public library systems,
the main library within an educational institution or the library of a
large industrial or research organization. Opening hours should
total at least 50 per week.

Deciding on levels of service

Deciding on levels of service, identified as the fourth in the series of
six first steps for a library service, will be crucial. It is at this point
that the expectations of library management have to be made clear,
the reasons for involvement fully understood, the training obligations accepted and participation within the local support networks
taken on board as an inescapable commitment.

For libraries working in an educational setting, the decision may
already have been accepted alongside the developments in learning
materials. All the implications or opportunities that can follow from
the increasing availability of materials and the growth in their use
could well suggest that a review of the service would be beneficial.
Such a review could prove opportune if other partners in the local
support networks need to develop or review their own services;
indeed, a joint review could provide the opportunity to improve
local services on a co-operative bases, whilst ensuring the most effective value for money, both for the providers concerned and for the
individual learners whom it is hoped to benefit.

In public libraries the decision-making process is perhaps rather
less clearly defined, involving, as it must, some very interesting
questions of principle and of public library purpose.

Although public libraries have a legal obligation to provide a comprehensive service, with the education remit being included within this, the obligation does not extend beyond the traditional book format. A modern service to the adult independent learner requires much more, not simply in terms of the materials concerned, but also from the support services of staff, equipment and premises. It may be argued that the 1964 Public Libraries and Museums Act is simply out of date, but this does not solve the very real question of principle behind the free library service when an extension is sought to include the breadth of modern learning materials. Many public library authorities have already moved substantially into non-book formats, notably audio cassettes and compact discs; a charge is usually made for these services, although exceptions are often made for audio books, at least for the blind and partially-sighted. Existing policy decisions may well provide a basis for consideration of the wider range of open learning materials, although the major argument in favour of maintaining the free library principle in this area of provision remains the fact that such a service is ideologically identical with that for which the public library service was created.

The decision in favour of providing this service must be followed up by one that determines the levels of service to be provided at each library; this will depend upon the resources available to commit to staff training, acquisition of stock, purchase of appropriate shelving and equipment and the nature of local support networks. It will also depend very much on another decision: the nature of staff involvement.

Staff involvement with adult learners raises two questions. The first is how, where and whether to differentiate between advice and information; the second is the quality control of information provided, with the potential risk of professional liability for the provision of wrong information. As far as the first question is concerned, it is possible to arrive at a fairly clear line by referring to the stages within the educational guidance process described in Chapter 3 and identifying the responsibility for service delivery against each element within it. This will then provide a clear focus for staff training programmes and a framework for the library service's position within the local support network. Quality and accuracy of information provision is an accepted responsibility for any chartered librarian within the Library Association's Code of Professional Conduct. This reponsibility is passed on to support staff through effective training programmes. Where information is being given to adult learners who seek to improve their career prospects or develop their business abilities this responsibility needs to be accepted, understood and practised by all involved in providing the service. By doing this in a positive manner it is possible to improve the quality of professional library service quite considerably, much to the benefit of the users, the reputation of the library service and the satisfaction of the individual members of staff who are actively involved.

The interrelated questions of advice, information and quality can also be considered in the context of total quality management and the requirements of British Standard 5750. Many organizations are now turning towards the accreditation offered by this standard, and the principles that lie behind it are being actively sought amongst industrial suppliers, a number of whom will be the potential clients for learning programmes through libraries.[24]

Working with the support network

Within any one locality there will be a number of organizations involved with adult learners, sometimes on a competitive basis. The library needs to be both aware of and in contact with each of them in some way or other, but preferably through a recognized consultative and support system. The organizations most likely to be involved are Training and Enterprise Councils, universities, polytechnics, colleges, local education authorities, public library services, youth and community services, careers services, trades unions, voluntary agencies (including the Workers' Educational Association, Women's Institutes, Townswomen's Guilds, and the University of the Third Age), job centres, commercial training organizations, regional offices of the Open University, community organizations and open learning centres. All are providers of guidance or learning opportunities, sometimes both.

The purpose of the support system has to be to provide access either for or on behalf of the adult independent learner to people who can help them in various ways, ranging from the provision of educational and vocational guidance to practical help with course work. It is also through the support system that librarians in different types of library within any one area are able to meet, work together and contribute their combined abilities and resources to the overall service.

The support system must begin with access to information, to ensure that providers of education of any type within an area can be aware of what each is offering, thus allowing libraries to fulfil the obligations to disseminate details of educational opportunities and to relate these to learning needs. It must then be in a position to advise and encourage learners and to help them with their aims and aspirations, to help them apply their learning towards meeting their personal objectives, to give them access to tutor support and, on occasions, to help them enter for examinations.

However, the support system should not exist simply for the adult independent learner, rather it should also exist for the providers themselves. The overall objective of such a system is to identify and meet the educational and training needs of local industry and commerce and of private individuals. The development of the framework of National Vocational Qualifications gives added impetus to the objective. In the process, efficient information and guidance systems will be needed, as will some degree of mutual agreement about course provision in more specialist subjects. These aspects can be assisted by participating in and being aware of the wider national open learning networks: the Open Learning Federation, for providers, and the British Association for Open Learning, representing producers.

Within the network there will be the core agencies – those with a primary involvement in local educational guidance and delivery – as well as the more general agencies, such as the trades unions or citizens' advice bureaux, which will be involved with a range of services, only some of which are educational. In addition, some outside specialist agencies may well become involved from time to time: bodies such as adult literacy referral services, the Materials and Resources Information Service (MARIS) or the Educational Counselling and Credit Transfer Information Service (ECCTIS).

The network is likely to involve regular (but not necessarily very frequent) meetings between senior members of staff from each of the providing bodies, supplemented by smaller and more specialized groups able to co-ordinate such matters as open learning, basic skills education or educational guidance. The groups may be semi-permanent or *ad hoc* according to the extent and nature of local needs, but they should provide the basis for individuals to work with each other on a relatively informal basis to solve specific problems for the benefit of individual learners.

A major advantage of the local support network, particularly from a library point of view, is its ability to contribute greatly to training programmes for library staff. The educational expertise that is available is frequently helpful in overcoming some of the possible barriers that develop when learning packages and their related services are introduced into libraries. Colleges will usually be pleased to make such expertise available to other bodies, although they may well make a charge for doing so . As a bonus it will normally be found that the training courses themselves help to establish good mutual relations and contribute to future developments.

In situations where a local network does not already exist it will be necessary to bring the various agencies together and for one of the bodies to take the lead. This has tended to be a responsibility undertaken by local education authorities,[25] but geographical considerations may sometimes make this difficult, as may changes arising from the Education Reform Act, local government reorganization and changes resulting from the varying influences of Training and Enterprise Councils. Library services may find that, at least initially, they should undertake the leading role in setting up the network, although the secretarial responsibility may well move between organizations over a period.

5. The materials

Multi-media choices

The materials of open learning range far beyond the traditional book, although this remains a base from which other activities develop. The book is still a major (although not always a constant) element in open learning provision; learning packages are now compiled using a variety of additional media, of which the following are some of the most popular:

- assignments;
- audio cassettes;
- case studies;
- computer programs;
- guides;
- management games;
- samples and materials;
- slides;
- study planners;
- video cassettes;
- workbooks and/or worksheets.

The most sophisticated packages make use of computer-based interactive video lessons, while the use of computer programs generally is fairly common.

The nature of these packages raises many questions in the minds of librarians seeking to acquire and manage them as part of normal lending library stock. Academic librarians have come to terms with the increasing range of learning resources over many years and can often offer colleagues in public libraries much useful guidance in their management, as does the particularly valuable work of the Audio-Visual Group of the Library Association. However, for any library embarking upon an active involvement in open learning the starting point has to be one of commitment to accepting this wide variety of media.

Basic stock decisions

Once the decision has been made to include open learning packs within the normal library stock a number of other decisions will need to follow about how the stock is to be displayed, what arrangements are to be made for selection and purchase, whether the stock is to be included within the main library catalogue, policies on the period of loan and on reservations and the need for supporting hardware. These decisions will also have a training implication for all the staff who will be administering and presenting the service to users.

Library users appreciate finding open learning areas identified clearly and separately within libraries. On the other hand, there are advantages in displaying multi-media packages alongside books and other material on the same subject, although the effective use of a comprehensive catalogue can overcome many aspects of this problem. Given the nature of some of the open learning materials, as well as their cost, some element of control and supervision is also to be recommended. As the extent to which a particular library is committed to open learning provision has to be taken into account in the way in which the service is presented, the decision about levels of service, detailed in the previous chapter, will be an important one. These levels are now used to look at service presentation in more detail.

Level 1. Contact point

Libraries providing a minimum level of open learning service are unlikely to carry much stock. Where stock is available it will usually be in the more popular subject areas and at the cheaper end of the market range, such as packs on the basics of foreign languages or the use of popular personal computers. In such cases the stock is best incorporated within the normal library subject sequence with perhaps one or two titles being displayed to draw attention to other information about the open learning services to which that particular library acts as a gateway.

The gateway function is one that must be looked at carefully. In order to act as an information point about learning opportunities, the library must stock a reference collection of literature and must display a current range of giveaway leaflets and brochures about the learning opportunities that are available within the wider community in which it is situated. This requirement places an obligation upon the library system involved to ensure that this stock is acquired and maintained. It is a function that is often aided by an effective local support network.

The literature collection should be supplemented by a well organized information board devoted entirely to learning opportunities and to the role played by the library service, particularly for the adult independent learner. This board will act as the signpost for the library's second function at this level: that of acting as a reception and referral point for open learning enquiries; it may also allow for a changing display of one or two open learning packs (with their useful 'enticement' value) in addition to the display of giveaway literature. Given the nature of the library involvement at this level, it is probable that the actual stock selection will be carried out elsewhere in the library system.

Level 2. Delivery centre

Where a library is fulfilling an active role as a delivery centre for open learning, it will expect to stock a basic collection of open learning packs. Here it will usually be most effective to keep the collection together, close to the enquiry and computer facilities which will be essential equipment in such a library. There can also be an advantage in advertising the availability of open learning packs within the normal subject sequences; this may be done with dummy packs which can be exchanged at the counter for the real thing, or by including a few 'tasters' in the more popular subjects within the main sequence.

41

The dummy pack approach has the advantage of increased security for expensive material; sometimes the same effect can be achieved by using the real outer pack without the more 'attractive' elements of its contents, these being inserted on issue.

The presentation of open learning materials is best achieved by face-forward display units, preferably associated with the information and guidance facilities, literature display and sales point for workbooks and supporting material. At this level of service a minimum display stock of 60 learning packs should be aimed for at any one time.

Level 3. Study centre

Study centre libraries will already hold substantial and wide-ranging stocks of both lending and reference materials. They will have study facilities and trained staff and the move towards the specific provision of open learning resources is likely to be a natural progression.

In the case of a library which is active as a full-scale study centre there will be a need for both reference and lending use of learning packs, but not necessarily separate reference and loan collections. Security of the collection is likely to be of some concern, especially if it contains (as it most likely will) a number of the more expensive packs and those which use computer material. Here there is a double need to guard against both loss of stock and corruption of data. There may also be questions to resolve about copyright, a matter likely to be of particular importance in public libraries. In study centre libraries there is a probability that open learning packs will be housed most effectively within the normal subject sequence, resorting to dummy packs where necessary to ensure security, although it is preferable to remove the vulnerable items and reinsert them on issue, if that is possible. Some duplication of stock may be required either to cater for demand in the more popular subject areas or to provide specific copies for reference use only. Libraries in this category should aim to have a stock of 150 learning packs available for loan at any one time with all of these capable of being reserved for reference use if required.

Library staff become involved with adult learners as they begin, progress and achieve personal study aims and ambitions. Frequently this will involve undertaking a rôle as mentor to the learner, offering advice on sources, encouragement to overcome hurdles and generally providing a stable source of knowledgeable support.

Wherever open learning is allocated a specific area within a library there will be a need to display samples at least of the stock available, unless the whole collection is housed at this point. Face-forward display shelving is usually the best for this purpose, and in some cases the type of face-forward periodical display shelves that provide storage space immediately behind can be useful. The shelving units should also permit the display of posters and promotional material, both to draw attention to the collection and to allow links to be established with other providers as well as with educational guidance support.

The study centre library will be a focal point for adult learning service delivery for a wide area or a large community; it will probably provide the co-ordination for stock selection and literature distribution to a number of other libraries offering lower levels of service, together with a high level of information and guidance support. This library will provide a Training Access Point (as long as the service is available within its area) co-ordinate stock selection requirements and provide a full range of links with tutors and the local support network.

Stock selection

The first requirement for the selection of stock is money. For the library service starting out in the field of open learning materials a basic rule of thumb calculation would be to allow an average cost of £50 per learning pack, although this average is liable to rise if the service is successful and demand is generated for more-advanced learning material. At 1992 prices[26] this would mean a minimum budget of £5000 to set up a library as a delivery centre and a minimum of £12,000 for a study centre. In each case it is wise not to spend the whole of that amount at once, but to keep back about one third of the allocation in order to respond to specific demands and to gain information from user feedback in order to develop the collection.

There will normally be an advantage in purchasing an initial stock of sufficient size and scope to permit a well publicized launch of the service to take place. This stock may be selected on the basis of the librarian's existing knowledge of the library and its users, but it will probably be more effective if a target group within the local community is also identified and some stock purchased accordingly. This approach can be very relevant when the library is working in partnership with other learning providers or with specific sources of funding, such as the Training and Enterprise Councils and Local Enterprise Companies.

Other points to consider will be the amount of tutorial support that a learning pack requires, and the source of that support. Some packs are sold complete with a defined level of support from the originating body, but this is usually on the assumption that it will only be used by one person. Where a library is lending the pack to a number of people, then it would be wise to identify either the additional cost of the extra support or local sources able to provide the same type of assistance. In both cases it is fairly certain that an additional cost will be involved, which is usually one to be borne by the adult independent learner.

Although it is not necessarily relevant for all types of library, the information about subject take-up revealed by the pilot projects funded in public libraries by the Employment Department is interesting.[27] The most popular subjects were:

- computing
- women returning to work
- office skills
- languages
- education and training
- accounting and bookkeeping

- health and safety
- basic skills
- GCSE subjects
- electrical skills
- management
- interviewing

However, these represent but a fraction of the total number of packages produced, which is now over 10,000. There are two major sources of information for librarians to use about the titles available. The first is the *Open learning directory*, published annually by Pergamon in conjunction with the Department of Employment, and the other is the British Association for Open Learning (BAOL), Standard House, 15 Hitchin Street, Baldock, Herts. SG7 6AL. BAOL represents producers and distributors of open learning materials and has a national network of delivery centres. These centres offer to librarians the opportunity to visit and inspect a range of currently available materials. Neither of these sources is comprehensive, nor is there a reliable reviewing service. The best way to select is to begin with the range of subjects to be represented; secondly, to draw up a list of criteria to which the learning pack must conform, and then to visit a centre which holds a reasonable collection and is able to offer independent advice and assessment. The criteria can be quite simple, such as:

- meeting a defined study level;
- packs for which extra copies of workbooks can be purchased (given that the library will wish to sell these);
- excluding packs which can be difficult to manage (such as the 120 miniature bricks in the *Learn about bricklaying* course;
- packs requiring low levels of tutor support.

In addition there may be criteria designed to assess the effectiveness of the learning pack. These would include:

- ensuring that objectives are clearly stated for both the whole course and each unit within it;
- checking the quality of audio and video material;
- looking at the structure of the course: manageable units, participation, feedback to the learner, maintaining interest;
- identifying the specific skills to be achieved by the end of the course;
- well designed workbooks.

Where such criteria are established it is important that they should be reviewed once the service is under way since experience may show that higher levels of tutor support can be arranged, or that 120 miniature bricks will pose no real problem at all. Similarly arrangements for selection should be reviewed, since this is a developing and changing market.

Collections of open learning materials are also to be found in local open learning centres and in the offices of Training and Enterprise Councils. Effective selection can make use of these collections, together with publishers' catalogues and on-line databases of learning materials, with MARISNET being particularly useful. It is possible to order titles separately from the publishers, some of whom will give good discounts, otherwise it can be quite cost effective to use an open learning delivery centre, most of which can be expected to negotiate reasonable discounts. These are listed in the *Open learning directory*.

Public librarians should note that there may be occasions when publishers refuse to supply public libraries with open learning materials, although this is not a significant problem.

Stock processing

Once the stock has been ordered, it is likely to take about a month for copies to be received. As with books, this figure can only be an overall average, so expect some items to take rather longer. An allowance then has to be made for library cataloguing and processing before the stock can appear on the shelf. When a new service is being planned this process must be taken into account and a realistic timescale allowed.

It has to be assumed that all open learning packs will be catalogued as part of normal library stock; indeed the majority of competent computer cataloguing programs should be able to handle this type of material. It will be helpful if the computer catalogue is able to distinguish these packs from other types of stock so that they may be printed out as a discrete list for promotional purposes, preferably within subject groupings. Similarly, the use of a keyword descriptor, such as 'open learning pack', is helpful to the users of opac terminals. The catalogue entry must list **all** the component parts of the learning pack, including practical kits. This list will also be required to accompany the pack when it is used for lending purposes, so that staff can check that all components are present on both issue and return.

The processing of stock for issue will need to make provision for the separate storage of vulnerable components, such as computer discs and videotapes. It will also be sensible to keep back-up copies of the software involved, and possibly of the videotapes as well. It can be helpful if packs which include software and which are to be made available for loan, are supplied with both $5^{1}/_{4}$ and $3^{1}/_{2}$ inch disks to accommodate variations in users' machines. If they are to be kept for reference only, then the size of disk must be checked to ensure that it is compatible with the library computer.

Tutor support

Reference has been made to the need to take requirements for tutor support into account when selecting stock. The availability of such support needs to be viewed as an extension of the library stock, since it is another source of information appropriate to the user's needs.

Not all adult independent learners will wish to become involved with formal education classes, although many will welcome the opportunity to approach a specialist if this can be done without any feeling of obligation. This is where the value of local support networks and the effectiveness of the information and guidance systems begin to be felt, with the process depending on the quality of the link between the learner and the library.

Tutor support as a one-off occasion makes considerable demands upon the specialists concerned, so it is helpful if potential calls upon this resource can be estimated, to some degree at least, before open learning packs which require high levels of tutor involvement are made available in a library loan collection. This assessment is likely to give some indication of the charges which may be made to learners undertaking any particular course. In many ways this is potentially good business for everybody concerned, including the library, which may be entitled to some commission. The details involved in making such arrangements must vary from one locality to another, but they certainly offer fertile ground for the support network concerned, especially where university, college and public libraries are all involved. The following guidelines are provided as suggestions to assist librarians in meeting the needs of the adult independent learner in this situation.

Librarians will be well placed to identify subject areas of student and learner demand, while colleges will be able to detail areas of specialist ability that could be made available. Where sufficient commonality of purpose is shown to exist in a locality it will be possible to identify open learning packs with tutor support that could meet the need. As long as this support can be made available locally there is the opportunity for a joint college/library marketing initiative to promote a more specialist course, with a fixed price for the added-value element of a personal tutor link.

On a different level there is likely to be a demand for tutor support related to learner needs. The first instance is that of encouragement and basic learning assistance, and here the librarian will be able to provide for most needs within the mentor role that must accompany full adult learning services. Then there is the frequently felt need for somebody to comment on, or to mark, specific assignments. This service could be provided on a fixed fee basis per assignment. Where learners feel the need for more specific levels of personal tuition and college courses are not available, or unsuitable, then it may also be possible to provide this level of support, albeit at an agreed hourly rate. It is unlikely that many learners would be able to take up such a service on a regular basis, therefore the arrangement would probably be restricted to specific areas of learning difficulty and would have to be negotiated on an individual basis.

Stock management

Control of open learning packs in libraries must be geared to insuring against loss or damage. For this reason many of the vulnerable components of both lending and reference copies of these packs need to be kept away from public access and be issued against a specific signature, for reference use, or borrower's ticket, for loan. This record should be kept after the pack is returned by the next borrower as an added check against unidentified damage. Storage facilities adjacent to the point of issue will certainly be necessary. Equipment for checking components will be required to investigate complaints about faulty materials.

Learning packs which feature practical kits (such as the building bricks referred to earlier) are often worth having in stock as long as the necessary checking can be accommodated within the loan process; these will require a detailed inventory slip to be checked on both issue and return.

The loan period for open learning material needs to be extremely flexible. In many situations it is reasonable to impose the library's normal loan period for the initial issue of a pack, since this will give the borrower sufficient time to ascertain whether it is right for her or his purpose. Where the pack is perceived to be relevant, the borrower ought to be able to negotiate a sensible period of loan related to the study time allocated for the pack and the period over which the borrower can reasonably be expected to find that time. This is not quite as simple as it all sounds since such an approach will inevitably raise policy questions about the duplication of stock for popular material, the approach to reservations, and the possible loss of income from long loan periods. One answer to the latter point is to impose a large fine for non-return at the end of the extended loan period.

In some libraries charges for this service will be considered in any case. The basis for the calculation of these charges will depend upon the nature of the library's parent body, but in educational institutions they may well be set to ensure a return on the investment over an agreed number of loans. In public libraries such charges are likely to be resisted, but the situation within a local network when inter-library loans are sought for this material will certainly need policy resolution before such loans can be arranged.

6. Library staff

Awareness, information and delivery

The effectiveness of services to adult independent learners always depends upon the quality of the very first contact that the learner has with a member of the library staff. Although this may seem a somewhat trite observation it is surprising just how often the person in most need manages to encounter the very newest staff recruit. Since many of the would-be learners can be hesitant and uncertain about the ability of the library to help them, it is vital to avoid any such uncertainty on the library side of the encounter. At the very least that first response should be confident and welcoming, even if the actual enquiry is passed on to other staff as it progresses.

In order to provide this level of effectiveness, any library must ensure various levels of competence in its staff. There are three such levels to aim for: those of awareness, information and full service delivery. This general principle of staff training is designed to allow library managers to identify a level of competence that each member of staff can be expected to attain in relation to every individual aspect of the complete range of services available from the whole library system. It accepts that an overall level of initial awareness develops into a wider information base and then to full training, requiring specific input accompanied by time and practical experience.

Developing the knowledge base is a vital prerequisite of the effective open learning service. The three levels of competence outlined above will now be discussed.

Awareness

The very first lesson in awareness, to be absorbed by a new member of staff on day one, is the well known and accepted principle that if you don't know you ask someone else. This has to be accompanied by the message that it is always a greater sin to try to hide ignorance than it is to confess it.

As far as adult learning needs and open learning provision are concerned, it is essential that all staff are aware of two things: first, that there is a service available; and secondly, that the library has literature about that service. In many libraries these facts will be stated in a staff manual which then offers further information about the way in which the service can be approached.

The level of awareness of library staff about the literature provision should extend to showing enquirers where this is displayed and to knowing what range of literature the library normally provides. However, the basic requirement is to ensure that any member of staff is able to demonstrate an awareness of this service that is appropriate at least to that expected at the contact point, or level 1, of service provision, as detailed earlier.

It is important to note that the level of awareness suggested does not extend to knowing and passing on to enquirers specific details of the service provided, particularly not as regards the availability of educational information and guidance. These are matters which require very specific levels of competence and should be dealt with by less-qualified or -experienced staff passing on enquiries to those who have the appropriate knowledge or training to provide the relevant information. At the awareness level it is valuable to demonstrate the dangers of becoming involved at a deeper level in a way which may be potentially unhelpful to would-be learners. Referral to the full range of services available, which will be detailed in the information handouts that staff are trained to provide at this level, should be sufficient.

Information

At the information level staff should have moved forward from the awareness stage to an understanding of the range of services available to the adult independent learner. Much of the required knowledge base will be that appropriate to a library providing a delivery centre type of service. In particular, all members of staff should be expected to understand the commitment of the library service to open learning and have a specific knowledge of the following:

- awareness of learners as definable library clients (see Chapter 2);
- library policy towards independent learners;
- the nature of adult independent learners and their needs;
- the scope of background information provided and the ways in which it is maintained;
- the range of stock and materials provided;
- the nature of the educational information and guidance services;
- the ways in which the service is managed and organized and levels of service provided, including how and when to refer to a library providing level three services.

The objective at this level of training is to ensure that all staff working within a library that offers quality services to adult independent learners are fully aware of the nature of those services, and of the way in which the library provides them. Frequently the staff concerned may not be those who provide the full depth of information and guidance, but complete familiarity with the nature, interests and problems of the learners and their materials is important for library staff at all levels to be able to understand and deploy.

Full service delivery

Staff who are expected to operate at this level of competence in providing library services to adult independent learners will normally be both professionally qualified and experienced. They will need an intimate knowledge of all aspects of the service and are likely to be fully involved in its management. As a result they will be able to:

- apply, promote and develop the library policy towards adult independent learners;
- show empathy with adult independent learners and their needs;
- identify, control and monitor the supply of background information relevant to independent learning;

52

- select and purchase a range of books and open learning materials appropriate to the interests of library users;
- contribute to and work within the local support network;
- personally provide educational information and guidance or know when to refer to more appropriate educational guidance;
- advise users on the library resources most appropriate to their needs;
- demonstrate the use of computers and other technology provided in the library for the support of adult independent learners and their needs;
- organize or take part in the training of other staff involved at all levels of service to adult independent learners;
- supervise other library staff who assist in providing adult and open learning services.

Training for competence

Since education and training are the purposes of service provision in the field of adult and open learning it should be self-evident that the competence of all staff involved in the delivery of such a service must be clearly demonstrated.

In a 1988 Research Report for the British Library[28] Linda Butler detailed a number of case studies and drew from them several lessons which had implications for the training of public librarians dealing with either potential or actual educational guidance enquiries. The lessons, quoted here, are worthy of note by all librarians since they emphasize the importance of not taking anything for granted when training for full competence in this field:

1. Enquirers may have little idea of what the library can offer and frequently fail to exploit its resources fully, by failing to ask the right questions or all the questions they could.

2. Enquirers vouchsafe little of the implications of their enquiry and librarians may sometimes fail to exploit opportunities to do so, thus diminishing the value of the contact for the enquirer.

3. Librarians make assessments of enquirers which may have substantial impact on the conduct and outcome of the enquiry.

4. Librarians attend to narrowing down an enquiry when for enquirers there may be a need to broaden it. Failure to do so, which is reinforced by inadequately displayed and manipulated browsing facilities, tends to reinforce enquirers' misconceptions rather than correcting them.

5. Enquirers may need help in recognizing their own advice and/or counselling need; when they are so aware they may need assistance in the way of accurate and assisted referral. Enquirers are often unaware of, or mistakenly dismiss (or indeed use) sources of help which may be very valuable to them.

Work in this subject area has the double dimension of being both library and educationally orientated, so training programmes need to reflect both aspects quite clearly. For an effective process this means working with other specialists, usually within the framework of the local support network.

The help and value of the local support network becomes more apparent when consideration is given to the available inputs to training in adult and open learning services. Two of the most important are those of the National Educational Guidance Initiative (NEGI), funded by the Department for Education and the Employment Department and set up by the Unit for the Development of Adult Continuing Education (amalgamated with the Further Education Unit in April 1992) and the Employment Department and its various divisions. NEGI has developed a current training strategy, while TEED, in its former incarnation as the Training Agency, has produced *Standards of performance for open learning staff*.

The aims of NEGI's training and educational guidance strategy are:[29]

- identify the training, learning and development requirements of educational guidance practitioners and managers;
- map training and staff development opportunities in relation to educational guidance;
- provide consultancy and advice on the content and context of educational guidance training programmes being planned or operated, and review their links with other training programmes in the guidance field;

54

- disseminate information relating to educational guidance training and staff development as widely as possible;
- ensure that educational is represented in all lead body negotiations and the subsequent development of occupational standards and qualifications in advice, guidance and counselling.

The Training Agency's statements of competence[30] are to:

- find and select open learning packages and programs;
- design and develop open learning programmes;
- provide advice and direction to learners;
- provide tutoring for individuals and groups of learners;
- provide administrative services for an open learning scheme;
- manage the resources of an open learning scheme;
- provide marketing services for an open learning scheme;
- evaluate and validate an open learning scheme and its programmes.

Both these sets of guidelines have become accepted, albeit in the somewhat different environments for which they were conceived. As a result they now form a basis for training in both colleges and Training and Enterprise Councils. When used in the library context, there are obviously areas of training and competence which are less relevant than others, but in the context of the local support network, librarians will find an understanding of the competences of fellow professionals to be of considerable assistance in their own relationships with adult learners. The Lead Body for Advice, Guidance and Counselling is expected to set competences in this field as part of the development of national vocational qualifications.

NEGI's remit covers consultancy and advice to help in the planning and development of training programmes for guidance workers and in the establishing of local networks for educational guidance.[31] Much of this advice is contained in the Initiative's publications, obtainable from:

National Educational Guidance Initiative
13 Wellington Road
Dewsbury
West Yorkshire, WF13 1HF
Telephone 0924-457400

Practical training schemes

A good place to start is by looking at some of the open learning training packs that have already been produced. The *Open learning directory* is a useful guide to these packs, with titles such as *Exploring open learning,The evaluation of open learning materials*, and *A-Z of open learning* all at the lower cost end of the range and requiring two or three hours of a person's time.

At an early stage in the development of the library service to adult learners it is important to hold awareness sessions for all staff who will be actively involved in any way. These sessions will include an explanation by senior library staff of the background and philosophy of the service, and talks by specialists from other parts of the local support network about their own contributions to it. An important part of such sessions is the opportunity to handle open learning packs and to gain experience of some of the technology involved. For staff at libraries providing a level one service, a short (half-day) course will be sufficient, although others will normally require a whole day.

The awareness courses will need to be followed up in two ways. First by on-the-job training at each library, with the purpose of emphasizing the points made at the awareness course and ensuring that the service gets off to a good start. Secondly, by in-depth courses for librarians who will be more closely involved with the learners.

Close involvement with the learners will arise both through the educational guidance process and the ongoing use of the library and its facilities. Much has already been said about the guidance process; at this stage practical training programmes for librarians who will be involved need to be set up on the lines already indicated, using local resources from the network and assistance from NEGI publications and consultancy if required.

The ongoing needs of the adult learners are a separate matter.

Apart from the calls for assistance in using library resources that canbe anticipated, there will also be the need to encourage contacts between learners and to provide links with tutors if required. The library should maintain a record for each learner and, with the learner's permission, will be able to use this to identify potential groups of learners who could meet together to offer mutual support and encouragement. The record of individual learning needs and achievement will also have other uses. In particular it will allow a librarian to act as a mentor to the learner, providing advice on progress, helping to anticipate learning needs that the library should respond to and generally undertaking the counselling, assessing and enabling roles enshrined within the guidance process. Librarians are basically well equipped to fulfil this role, but most need specific training and encouragement in order to do so successfully.

In addition to the help that can be found in the publications of NEGI and the Employment Department, already referred to, the report *Open learning and public libraries*[32] pays tribute to the helpfulness of local colleges and open learning centres in the organization of training courses, while Clwyd County Library has produced its own training pack entitled *Learn with your library*.[33] Gloucestershire County Library's report *GOLD in the Forest of Dean*[34] also gives some information on training programmes, as does the training awareness pack on the subject, issued by the National Council for Educational Technology in 1987.[35]

There is a qualification course, parts of which are suitable for librarians who become involved with an adult learning service at level three, or who spend a significant proportion of their time working with learners. The Award for the Development and Delivery of Flexible and Open Learning (ADDFOL) is made by the Scottish Vocational and Education Council, City & Guilds and the Royal Society of Arts, and there are at least three distance learning courses, in addition to any local college courses which may be available.

7. Marketing the service

The reasons why

In today's society marketing plays a considerable role in defining the perceptions of would-be users about the ability of any service to deliver what it promises. Libraries have for long tended to assume that many purposive users already know what services are available, although this would not seem to be a perception borne out by user surveys. At the same time there is often the concern that to advertise library services may simply add to a burden of service that is already proving difficult to deliver – a situation which is likely to worsen as universities and colleges seek to respond to government initiatives to increase the numbers of students, without at the same time adding to library resources, and as public libraries find increasing difficulty in maintaining a comprehensive service as resources decline.

Despite these concerns, a programme of marketing library services for learners, and of promoting the media of open learning must be undertaken. The main reason for taking this approach is that it is a follow-on from the policy decision to provide these services made in the expectation that they will meet a market need. In some situations adult and open learning may be seen as a logical progression from earlier provision, while in the case of public libraries they may be seen both as a valuable contribution to the comprehensive library service which there is a legal obligation to provide, and as a politically worthwhile endeavour.

Marketing is by no means synonymous with advertising, although advertising will certainly be required to some extent at least. In this context marketing is the promotion of a library service amongst the community which it is believed will benefit from its availability. The process has to begin with the 'product' that is being marketed, which must be identified quite clearly in the minds of the providers before it can be promoted at all. The practice of giving a specific service a name, the initials of which form an acronym, is a popular (and some might say overdone) approach to creating such an identity. Examples abound of acronyms being used to describe services of all types, but one particularly inspired creation is useful to demonstrate the effectiveness of the approach.

Gloucestershire County Library was one of ten public library authorities to receive funding from the Employment Department in 1990 'to establish an open learning service that offers members of the public access to open learning programmes on terms that are attractive to unsponsored individuals'.[36] This was a new service that was seen as having benefits for many existing library users and, more importantly, for many people who did not use the library service at all; the benefits had to be marketed, the service had to be established amongst staff and users alike, and the timescale to achieve all this was really quite short. A name for the service was decided upon, which on the face of it is fairly uninspiring: the Gloucestershire Open Learning Desk. However, when shortened to the initial letters and with the addition of the national library symbol and some graphics, then the result became:

This device was most effective. It immediately suggested something very desirable; it was something for the library to be proud of, and for its users to want; publicity material was usually guaranteed to receive rather more than a cursory glance and, above all, the service had an aura of quality (which was enhanced by the publicity material) that required all involved with it to do their best to live up to a high standard of service.

A marketable service

The lesson of the Gloucestershire example is that, to be effective in marketing, it is necessary to market benefits that the targeted users can appreciate rather than items of library stock and service. For services to adult learners examples of such benefits are:

- modern learning methods;
- acquiring new skills;
- lifeline for women would-be returners;
- positive pursuit of leisure interests;
- better qualifications, leading to:
    career development;
    job satisfaction;
    higher income;
    improved status;
- personal convenience.

By looking at the service in this way it is possible to motivate staff as well as to encourage users. Once the service has an identity and a purpose it is then necessary to move on to presenting and publicizing it. Furthermore, the same approach can be taken to the promotion of the library as the vehicle for undertaking study in this way. The points to concentrate on are essentially those detailed in Chapter 4:

- convenient community location;
- reasonable opening hours;
- availability of study space;
- trained and qualified staff;
- help in selecting courses and materials;
- liaison with tutors and other learners.

Having decided upon the positive aspects of the service that need to be marketed, the next move must be to decide to whom these services should be marketed. In Chapter 2 the range of potential adult independent learners is set out, but it is not necessary to attempt to target all of them at the same time; indeed, the service may well prove more effective if a specific group is identified to receive the service, certainly while it is new and needing to find its feet. In any case, demand from individual would-be learners will occur once the service is underway, and other specific groups will continue to be identified as the service progresses.

Publicity

Publicity is hard work: it is hard work for the librarian since nobody else is likely to do it. There are likely to be people who can help, but the impetus has to come from the person who is responsible for the service, who believes in it and who wants to tell others about it.

Publicity is not just about producing leaflets, although that is a good place to start. It is about telling as many people as possible about your service, and telling them in a way which will make it sound as attractive to them as you know it to be. The good news about publicity is that it is frequently 'free' in so far as newspapers and periodicals will usually be glad to use pictures, stories and information sent to them, while the launch of a new service can often attract radio and television interest as well. Where it is possible to provide copy in the form of a 'human interest' story success is even more likely.

A good publicity programme will include:

- an attractive basic information leaflet about the service, and a distribution programme for it;
- a list of press and media outlets from which you hope to get publicity, using named editors or journalists, wherever possible.
- a press launch of the service, preferably by a local personality and accompanied by: an informative press release (about 250 words) before the event; pictures of the event immediately after it has taken place, with a revised press release;
- displays in the library, including an interactive video, if possible.
- a booklet giving details of the open learning packages available from the library service;
- a forward plan of service developments, with both service and publicity objectives for each one;

- regular news stories about progress;
- awards to successful learners;
- links with other services.

It is very easy to forget about organizing the publicity programme until the last minute. This is a mistake. A good publicity programme is likely to increase the chances of success quite considerably, and consequently it should be planned alongside the development of the whole service. In this way it can be used to help progress, by emphasizing that the new service is becoming accepted, by recounting stories about its users and by generally indicating success. The integration of publicity into the development in this way produces a momentum, an interest and, all being well, a self-fulfilling prophecy. At the same time the integration of staged service and publicity objectives, which can be flexible, should prevent the service from committing the classic error of first advertising a product and then finding that demand is so great that the service cannot be delivered effectively.

The wider market

So far the emphasis in this chapter has been on marketing the service to learners solely within the library context. There is also a need to market the service to a range of organizations that may be linked with the library or may be completely outside it; in addition the service can be marketedwithin related fields of activity.

The first organization to target for effective marketing of the library's service to adult independent learners has to be its parent body. Nearly every library operates within a host organization, whether it be a university, a college, an industrial or commercial company or a local authority. This body holds the purse strings. The objective of marketing the library's work in the field of open and flexible learning to the host organization has to be to show the library's effectiveness and its value to the organization, and thus to justify continuity of funding or, even better, an increase in budget. The library's motives in providing this type of service are certain to be dictated by a desire to provide a service that is most appropriate to the needs of the library users. These users are the same people as those for whom the organization as a whole has a concern, so the marketing exercise is necessary to ensure awareness of the work of the library and to show that the services provided are up-to-date and relevant.

Marketing to the parent body means involving such people as directors, governors, committee chairmen, chief executives and senior managers in specific promotional activities, and inviting them to the launch of the new open learning service. It also means making sure that press releases and photographs are included in house journals, particularly when pictures have been taken which include one or more of the influential people within the organization. The stories of the successes that develop as the service progresses will continue to maintain a high profile for the library, especially where these successes can be shown to emphasize the corporate objectives of the organization.

Convincing members of the parent body of the usefulness and value of services to learners and of the provision of open and flexible learning packages will be a valuable step in the promotion of this service to related organizations, as well as, on occasions, to other sections of the library's own organization. There is a degree of overlap and interaction between members of governing bodies of all types, and a few friends amongst them can be of immense value to any library service.

Marketing library services in the field of education in general, and for the adult independent learner in particular, to people and organizations who have little or no connection with the library will mean addressing a few basic questions and presenting the answers in a way that will appeal to the motivations of potential users of the services. This can often be achieved most effectively within the local network which is able to provide constructive criticism, outside viewpoints and access to expertise. Librarians need to present their services in the light of what, why and how adults prefer to learn and what barriers are perceived to exist to prevent this happening. For libraries operating outside the academic environment it may also be necessary to show that they too are as aware, as lively and as interesting as college activities are often perceived to be, not least by the world of industry and commerce which is increasingly a purchaser of educational products.

In this context, specific publicity efforts need to be made to promote the ability of the library as a training provider amongst the members of the local Training and Enterprise Councils or Local Enterprise Companies. Here the links with career services, with training access points and existing business information services will all be important. Once again these possibilities emphasize the importance of the library establishing its position within the local network as so many of the contacts can develop from the acceptance of the library as a full and valid partner on the local education and training scene.

Finally consideration needs to be given to publicizing the learning facilities of libraries in places where people with learning needs can be found. This involves making contact with clubs and societies, youth organizations and small firms, giving talks or demonstrations and leaving information on notice boards and in staff rooms.

The library environment

The motivation of library users can be dissipated by a poor library environment; for non-users a good library environment is absolutely necessary if the publicity about the service is to stand a chance of being believed. Where the environment is seen as inadequate, even the slightly hesitant potential learner will walk away without even asking that first basic question

Adult independent learners want libraries that are appealing and interesting, pleasant and efficient to work in, effective and supportive. In some libraries such an environment has to be created alongside the more easy-going atmosphere of a community focus, which itself can be a strong publicity attraction.

Non-users often judge libraries on hearsay. This evidence can well be favourable, provided that the library has offered good service to the individual being consulted. It may also by quite unfavourable, perhaps on the basis of a single poor experience. There is an increasing likelihood that the service will be judged in the first instance against the criteria that have been absorbed from the commercial world, where high standards of presentation are often equated with equally high standards of service. Certainly, they encourage it, whilst quality training programmes invariably ensure that reality matches expectation. Libraries have to be seen in just the same way, and some care and attention to this aspect of marketing the service must be seen as having high importance and high priority.

Libraries that are hard to find, that look institutional or unwelcoming, can hardly expect to attract very many new users. Attention has to be paid to signposting in the street, so that people can find the building easily, and to making the building's function obvious to the person approaching it. Some indication on the outside of the building of the services offered inside can also be most helpful, particularly if these include access to technical facilities, such as fax or word processing, that will attract custom. Although it is no longer possible to assume that passers-by know what the word 'library' can really mean in a modern society, few libraries clearly indicate anything approaching the whole range of information, reference and lending services that can be found within the building, let alone mention adult learning or educational guidance. Many post offices now display their services in this way, and libraries could well follow suit to encourage new users, including, of course, many potential adult independent learners.

On entering the building the reception facilities must be equally welcoming in order to maintain the good impression that it is hoped has already been created. Reference has been made earlier to the need to display open learning materials effectively, and the same applies to the whole library, which is a learning experience in itself. Good guiding, reasonable allocation of study space and accommodation for the equipment provided in support of adult learning activities will also help to foster the welcoming atmosphere, which may be rounded off by providing a coffee machine, or even a coffee shop in large library buildings.

When this has been achieved, or nearly so, there is one more aspect to effective marketing of services for adult learners. This is to ensure that the continuous monitoring of services and learning needs provides a feedback not simply into the provision of stock or the improvement of information and guidance, but also into the continuing promotion of the adult learning service. One-off publicity efforts will not be enough; the library has to be regarded as a part of the local adult education scene, with new courses being featured in local literature in just the same way as are the more formal classes in subjects such as languages, literature, motor mechanics or computer programming. The development of customer charters for open learning is an impending move that will contribute to the monitoring and feedback processes.

8. Assessment and evaluation

An essential element

Any aspect of library service requires regular monitoring and feedback if it is to continue to respond effectively to its users and, just as importantly, to convince its non-users. Sometimes it can be difficult to obtain an objective evaluation, particularly from the current users of a service, for reasons which include both low expectations and the fear that assessment may be the precursor of reform, or even abandonment, of the service being enjoyed. From a library standpoint, however, assessment and evaluation of services is something to be welcomed, especially when a new, or relaunched, service is involved. Such evaluation will be a prerequisite for any open learning services developed in conjunction with funding from the Employment Department, Training and Enterprise Council or Local Enterprise Company.

The monitoring of a targeted service to learners should be seen a an important component within such provision. When the service includes the availability of open learning materials, supported by educational information and guidance, it is absolutely essential. This type of service, with its intimate involvement with the individual learners, is ideally placed to provide honest feedback. If such feedback is collected and analysed it can only be of benefit to the continued effectiveness of this aspect of library service.

Another significant reason for undertaking monitoring of services is that the process can both improve the service itself and enhance staff morale at the same time. So often in libraries people express thanks for a service provided, inducing a general 'feel good' mood for the recipient of the thanks. Specific examples of the real value of a service are harder to come by and a deliberate programme of performance assessment and evaluation will usually produce concrete evidence of achievement. It is also likely to reveal examples of inadequacy; but these are easier to accept (and thus lead to attempts to rectify) when ameliorated by the reality of overall success.

Having identified the opportunities it is also appropriate to utter a word of warning. In the enthusiasm for evaluation it is possible to become carried away into unnecessary levels of complexity. The best approach is always to keep things as simple as possible, ensuring that all the statistical information collected is as concise and as pertinent as can be achieved. The one approach that is to be recommended in the field of adult independent learning and the use of open learning materials is that of asking the users themselves to provide the assessment, either chosen from a sample frame or as part of the regular provision of the service. This method was used successfully in the evaluation of the Employment Department's public library pilot projects[37] and can also demonstrate some of the ways in which the local network is able to show benefit from its mutually supportive activities. Two examples from the different cases quoted by John Allred in a second follow-up to the projects[38] illustrate the point:

> A lady borrowed a creative writing pack of which she completed less than a half and, with hindsight, said it was not what she wanted anyway. However she had been given confidence in her ability to learn again by the librarian (who was an ex-Open University student and knew what open learning felt like) and decided to pick up on chemistry, a subject she had liked and mastered, at school. The library had put her in touch with the local college as a matter of routine and she used this contact to negotiate a place on a course in chemistry.
>
> A college lecturer tried out management teaching material to see how it compared with courses at his college – poorly he thought. Nevertheless he realised that material like this would be eminently suitable for staff training where staff members were unwilling to reveal their shortcomings, and who therefore wanted to learn in private. He is investigating material for in-service training of lecturing staff.

These cases also suggest other lessons which might be learnt from the users' experiences (such as the danger of too narrow a definition of desirable outcomes) and both point up the need for the library to keep a record of each learner and her or his progress whenever possible. Such records can be initiated during the educational guidance process, with learners being encouraged to discuss their learning experiences and needs on subsequent visits to the library. These records would include customary details of name, address and telephone number, as well as information about the date and time (morning, afternoon or evening) when the enquiry was made and analysis by age group, sex and employment status. The record would include prompts for librarians taking learners through the various guidance steps with notes of the identified needs and the action taken to meet them. This evaluation can be helped by asking users to complete an assessment of each learning pack that they use, thereby providing librarians with the opportunity to use these assessments separately to look at the effectiveness of the stock purchase programme. Wherever possible, the record should be confidential between the librarian as a mentor and the learner, with any analysis of the feedback excluding the possibility of identifying the learner.

Evaluation by objectives

Six first steps were suggested in Chapter 1 for a library service seeking to make provision for open learning. These steps are a convenient base from which to set objectives for the service in a specific library or group of libraries. This process is helped by the earlier definition of levels of service being provided. Once the objectives are set the resources needed to meet them will be identified by the library. These resources are likely to be finance led against the four elements of:

• staff • premises • equipment • stock

As the extent of the service is bound to be constrained by the amount of finance available it is necessary to ensure that the assessment process provides evaluation of costs against the returns obtained. Whilst such an evaluation can remain purely statistical, such as the number of packs purchased or the number of staff hours involved, it will also be necessary to evaluate the quality of service in relation to cost. This can be done by using the feedback from the learners themselves.

The objectives now provide the basic format for evaluation:

1. A *commitment to education* as a priority objective for the library service must show itself as an integral part of the service, reflected in a corporate understanding that is manifested through the processes of stock selection and assistance to readers, as well as in formal statements of policy and practice; all these will be reinforced by the staff training programme.

2. A *commitment to the adult independent learner* was identified through the provision of a specifically individual service that the user should find to be professionally efficient and competent. Where the decision has been made, then the service levels will have been extended to include educational information and guidance and access to open learning materials.

3. A *commitment to levels of service* at individual libraries, through the provision of defined levels of stock, study facilities and staff support, will have been made at the outset. Indications of tangible results will be needed to justify continued resourcing of the service and to direct its development.

These commitments can be evaluated both statistically and through the use of feedback (including the experiences of the staff).

Statistical records

Most of the statistics required can be collected fairly easily as part of the contact with users. Some may appear a little more difficult, depending upon local circumstances, but these can often be done on a sample basis. Others will simply be collected once a year as part of the annual assessment of the service. The following figures are suggested:

Subject	Statistic	Service level		
Information	Number of courses advertised	1	2	3
	Number of leaflets distributed	1	2	3
Guidance	Number of initial enquiries	1	2	3
	– staff time (0–2min,3–5min,etc)	1	2	3
	Number of learners counselled		2	3
	– staff time		2	3
	Number of registered learners		2	3
Network	Number of referrals			3
	Number of meetings			3
	– staff time (hours spent)			3
Stock	Target shelf stock		2	3
	Actual shelf stock (monthly)		2	3
	No. of items on loan (monthly)		2	3
	Total number of items lent	1	2	3
	(count once, not every 3–4 wks)			
	Average length of loan		2	3
	Sales of workbooks – income		2	3
Study	Area available		2	3
	Equipment provided		2	3
	No. of users (booking system?)		2	3
Training	No. of staff trained by level	1	2	3
	Costs of training	1	2	3
	– in house staff time			
	– bought-in training			

In conclusion

Quality services for adult independent learners cannot be provided cheaply, although they can be provided most cost-effectively. Simply by looking at the various elements that may be analysed from the above statistics it becomes obvious that this is not a service to be commenced without a reasonable term commitment. A period of at least three years is needed if there is to be an objective evaluation of results against investment. The latter has to be considerable at the outset of the service and needs to be costed against the benefits over a longer period than just the financial year in which the service is launched.

From the point of view of the adult independent learner this long- term commitment is essential. There are now many cases where people with a need for basic education have approached libraries tentatively, have been helped and guided through that level and on to advanced level studies and beyond. It is difficult to calculate the value of such a result either to the individual or to society as a whole in purely financial terms, but it is not nearly so difficult to show value for money when case studies are set against the overall investment.

9. Summary guidelines

Commitment

Library services, whether industrial, commercial, academic or public should accept involvement in adult independent learning services by:

- making a commitment to education as a priority objective;
- deciding to include open learning materials as part of the library stock;
- determining to provide a specifically individual service to each adult independent learner;
- identifying the level of service to be provided at each service point;
- ensuring that the levels of service available are clear to the user and fully understood by staff;
- ensuring that individual levels of service are found by the user to be professionally efficient and competent;
- participating in the local support network.

Awareness of learners

- Libraries should identify learners as definable clients who are individual, engaging in specific learning activities, self-motivated and managing their time effectively.
- In seeking to serve learners, libraries will identify broad groupings as an aid to service delivery:
  - self-employed business people;
  - women-returners;
  - 'second chance' for educational qualifications;
  - people unable to fit into formal course patterns;
  - retired people.
- Librarians, in acting as mentors to adult independent learners, will need to:
  - encourage, guide and motivate;
  - assist learners to record progress;
  - evaluate individual needs and abilities.
- For each learner the librarian must identify:
  - the specific subject to be studied;
  - the hoped-for level of attainment;
  - the current level of study skills;
  - the most appropriate study media;
  - guidance needs;
  - current or potential links with educational institutions.
- Libraries must be prepared to help learners who need to revise or develop both study and information skills.

Educational guidance

The seven parts of educational guidance strategy must be accepted by libraries, which should undertake the following activities:

- Informing, by:
  - producing literature about adult learning opportunities within the library;
  - maintaining comprehensive collections of leaflets about educational opportunities;
  - providing access to databases of learning opportunities.

- Advising, by:
  - providing staff at a clearly defined point of enquiry who can relate to adult learning needs;
  - helping learners to use library stock, catalogues and bibliographies;
  - guiding learners in the setting of their learning activities and objectives.
- Counselling, by providing staff trained to work with clients to help them discover, clarify, assess and understand their learning needs.
- Assessing, by training staff to develop a trusting, but informal, relationship between the independent learner and the library and thus to help the learner to appreciate her or his own level of ability.
- Assessing the information and study skills of learners and providing programmes to meet their needs.
- Enabling learners to obtain the best learning outcome by offering support and working with other agencies in the local support network.
- Representing the learner and advocating his or her needs to institutions and agencies.
- Feeding back to both learner and provider information on inadequately met learning needs.

Service level 1
Libraries offering a very basic service at this level will:
- act as an information point about learning opportunities, displaying literature and notices;
- be a referral point for open learning enquiries;
- act as a delivery and collection point for the loan and return of open learning materials;
- display sample learning materials.

Service level 2
As delivery centres for adult independent learning and open learning materials libraries at this level will:
- stock a basic collection of open learning materials;
- provide flexible loan arrangements;
- make study facilities and appropriate equipment available;

- Provide trained staff and a basic level of educational guidance with access to in depth guidance when required.

Service level 3
Study centre libraries are fully committed to the provision of open learning services and to assisting the adult independent learner by:
- stocking a wide range of open learning materials for loan and reference;
- maintaining reference and giveaway literature collections;
- providing in depth study facilities and equipment;
- offering a full educational guidance service;
- giving access to local networks and tutor support;
- acting as a centre of excellence for a wide area.

Local support network
Libraries of different types involved in adult independent learning within any one area must support one another in providing services to individual learners, and work with adult education providers to do so. The network should:
- be organized by an agreed lead practitioner and include representatives from all interested parties;
- enable learners to gain access to tutors and/or specialist sources;
- provide in depth guidance when required;
- identify the full range of local services required;
- meet the educational development needs of commerce and industry;
- make links with voluntary agencies;
- support staff training programmes;
- co-ordinate adult education provision.

Stock
- Adult independent learners must have access to a wide range of open learning materials.
- Selection should be undertaken by staff who are working with learners and their needs.
- Selection should be made from actual materials.

- Workbooks should be made available for sale.
- Stock should be available for inter-library loan.

Staff
- Adult independent learning services demand fully qualified and trained staff working directly with users.
- All staff should be aware of services to adult independent learners and of the literature about them.
- Librarians working in this field should be encouraged to acquire the Award for the Development and Delivery of Flexible and Open Learning (ADDFOL).

Equipment
When providing a full adult independent learning service libraries must have:
- playback equipment for working with video and audio tapes;
- microcomputers (for both learning programs and interactive video);
- word processing and spreadsheet facilities;
- slide viewer;
- photocopier.

Marketing
A marketing programme is essential and must emphasize:
- benefits for learners;
- usefulness of the library;
- value of service to parent body;
- regular publicity.

Assessment
- A long term commitment is essential when embarking upon a service to adult independent learners, therefore assessment should take this into account.
- Statistics should be amplified by user sampling methods to provide effective performance indicators.

References

Note: Full bibliographical details appear in the bibliography on page 79.

1. *Second Chance Centre:* the final report , [1992].
2. Vernon Smith. *Public libraries and adult independent learners,* 1987.
3. *People, jobs and opportunity,* 1992.
4. *How to profit from open learning:* company evidence [to the] Employment Department, [1990].
5. John Allred and Peggy Heeks. *Open learning and public libraries,* 1990.
6. Jane Straw. *International literacy year, 1990:* report on behalf of the Adult Literacy and Basic Skills Unit, 1991.
7. Adult Literacy and Basic Skills Unit. *The work of ALBSU with libraries,* 1992.
8. *People, jobs and opportunity,* 1992.
9. *ALBSU Newsletter,* no. 41, Spring 1991.
10. *People, jobs and opportunity,* 1992.
11. Unit for the Development of Adult Continuing Education (UDACE). *The challenge of change,* 1986.
12. Allred and Heeks. *Op.cit.*
13. UDACE. *Op.cit.*
14. *Using learning information.* 1990.
15. UDACE. *Op.cit.*
16. *Ibid.*

17. *Ibid.*
18. Library Association. *Code of professional conduct.*
19. UDACE. *Op.cit.*
20. *Ibid.*
21. *Ibid.*
22. Carole Barnes and John Allred. *Educational guidance for adults and public libraries*, 1991.
23. Linda Butler. *Case studies in educational guidance for adults*, 1984.
24. Vivienne Rivis and Jackie Sadler. *The quest for quality in educational guidance for adults*, 1991.
25. UDACE. *Op.cit.*
26. *The open learning directory, 1992.*
27. Allred and Heeks. *Op.cit.*
28. Linda Butler. *The rôle of public libraries in the provision of educational guidance for adults*, 1988.
29. NEGI. *Training and educational guidance* . Internal document, 10 Oct.1991.
30. Training Agency. *Standards of performance for open learning staff*, [1989].
31. National Educational Guidance Initiative. *[Promotional leaflet].*
32. Allred and Heeks. *Op.cit.*
33. Clwyd County Council. Library and Information Service. *Learn with your library*, 1990.
34. Hartridge, Digby. *GOLD in the Forest of Dean*, 1991.
35. Council for Educational Technology. *Training awareness pack* [published to accompany *Public libraries and adult independent learners*], 1987.
36. Training Agency. Tender document for an open learning service in public libraries, 1989.
37. Allred and Heeks. *Op.cit.*
38. John Allred. *Open learning and public libraries: report of the second follow-up of learners — fifty telephone interviews.* August 1990.

Bibliography

Adult learning & libraries news. (3 issues a year, free.) The Library Association, 7 Ridgmount Street, London, WC1E 7AE.

Adult Literacy and Basic Skills Unit. *The work of ALBSU with libraries.* London, ALBSU, 1992. (Typescript.)

ALBSU newsletter. (Quarterly.) Adult Literacy and Basic Skills Unit, 229/31 High Holborn, London, WC1V 7DA.

Allred, John, *and* Heeks, Peggy. *Open learning and public libraries: evaluation of a Training Agency initiative, by the Library Association for the Training Agency.* {Sheffield}, Training Agency, 1990. ISBN: 0 86392 352 6.

Allred, John. *Open learning and public libraries: report of the second follow-up of learners - fifty telephone interviews.* August 1990. (Typescript.)

Barnes, Carole, *and* Allred, John. *Educational guidance for adults and public libraries: report of the 1989/90 survey undertaken by the National Educational Guidance Initiative and the Library Association.* Leicester, National Institute of Adult Continuing Education on behalf of the Unit for the Development of Adult Continuing Education, 1991. ISBN: 1 872941 81 8.

Butler, Linda. *Case studies in educational guidance for adults.* Leicester, National Institute of Adult Continuing Education, 1984. ISBN: 0 900559 48 9.

Butler, Linda. *The rôle of public libraries in the provision of educational guidance for adults.* (British Library, Library and Information Research Report 22.) London, British Library, 1988. ISBN: 0 7123 3032 1.

79

Clwyd County Council Library and Information Service. *Learn with your library: a guide to effective learning for users and staff.* Mold, Clwyd County Council, 1990. ISBN: 0 904449 79 3.

Council for Educational Technology. *Training awareness pack.* London, CET, 1987. (Published to accompany 'Public libraries and adult independent learners' by Vernon Smith, *q.v.*)

Dale, S. *Guidelines for training in libraries, 8: distance learning.* London, The Library Association, 1986.

The Development of higher education into the 1990s; presented to Parliament by the Secretary of State for Education And Science.London, HMSO, 1985. (Cmnd.9524.)

Dolan, John, *and* Barrett, Jane. 'Libraries and educational guidance: a partnership for quality.' *Library Association Record,* **89** (7) 1987, 330-2.

Educational guidance news. (Quarterly.) Further Education Unit, Citadel Place, Tinwort h Street, London SE11 5EH.

Fisher, Raymond K. *Library services for adult continuing education and independent learning.* (Library Association pamphlet 40.) London, Library Association Publishing Ltd., 1988. ISBN: 0 85365 608 8.

Hartridge, Digby. *GOLD in the Forest of Dean; an open learning project centred on Cinderford Library:* report produced for the Training, Enterprise and Education Directorate. Gloucester, Gloucestershire County Library, Arts & Museums Service, 1991. ISBN: 0 904950 76 X.

How to profit from open learning - company evidence. Sheffield, Employment Department, [1990].

Hunt, Malcolm, *and* Bergen, Chris. EECTIS on CD ROM. Coventry,National Council for Educational Technology, 1991. ISBN: 1 85379 145 8.

International Literacy Year, 1990: report compiled and written by Jane Straw on behalf of the Adult Literacy and Basic Skills Unit (ALBSU). London, ALBSU, 1991. ISBN: 1 870741 28 5 .

Lewis, Roger. *How to tutor and support learners.* (Open learning guide no.3.) London, Council for Educational Technology, 1984.

The Library Association. *Code of professional conduct.* (in 'Yearbook'.)

The Open learning directory, 1992. Oxford, Pergamon, 1992. ISBN: 0 08 041805 8.

People, jobs and opportunity: presented to Parliament b y the Secretaries of State for Employment, Scotland and Wales. (Cm.1810). London, HMSO, 1992. ISBN: 0 10 118102 7.

Rivis, Vivienne. *Guidance for adult learners: the new challenges - towards a national strategy.* Leeds, Unit for the Development of Adult Continuing Education, 1992.

Rivis, Vivienne, *and* Sadler, Jackie. *The quest for quality in educational guidance for adults.* Leicester, National Institute of Adult Continuing Education on behalf of the National Educational Guidance Initiative of the Unit for the Development of Adult Continuing Education, 1991. ISBN: 1 872941 77 X.

[Scottish] national guidelines on open learning. Glasgow, Scottish Council for Educational Technology, 1989. ISBN: 0 86011 136 9,

Second chance centre: the final report [of] a joint project between Clwyd County Council Education Department and Library and Information Service. Rhyl (Clwyd), Rhyl Library, [1992].

Smith, Vernon. *Public libraries and adult independent learners: a report.* London, Council for Educational Technology, 1987. (Working paper no.27.) ISBN: 0 86184 173 5.

Surridge, Ronald, *and* Bowen, Judith. *The Independent Learning Project: a study of changing attitudes in American public libraries.* Brighton, Public Libraries Research Group, 1977. ISBN: 0 9503801 3 X.

Training Agency. *Ensuring quality in open learning: handbook for action..*Revised edition. Sheffield, Training Agency, 1990. ISBN: 0 86392 286 4.

Training Agency. *Standards of performance for open learning staff: an interim framework.* Sheffield, Training Agency, [1989].

Unit for the Development of Adult Continuing Education. *The challenge of change: developing educational guidance for adults.* Leicester, National Institute of Adult Continuing Education, 1986. ISBN: 0 900559 54 3.

Unit for the Development of Adult Continuing Education. *Delivering educational guidance for adults: a handbook for policymakers, managers and practitioners.* Leicester, National Institute of Adult Continuing Education, 1989. ISBN: 0 900559 84 5.

Using learning information: a guide to handling information in education and training databases. London, ADSET, 1990. ISBN: 0 863923 60 7.

Willetts, David. *Open learning in public libraries: a practical guide to implementing open learning.* Baldock (Herts.), British Association for Open Learning, for the Employment Department, 1991.

Index

82

Customer charters, 65

Delivery centres, 32–3
Department for Education, 54
Distance learning, defined, 2

Education, as objective, 3, 6, 69
Education Reform Act, 38
Educational background, 11
Educational Counselling and Credit
    Transfer Information Service
    (ECCTIS), 37
Educational guidance, 19–29, 33, 34
    definition, 19–20
    statistics, 70
    summary guidelines, 73
    training of library staff, 53–6
Employment Department, 7, 17, 20, 44,
    54, 57, 59, 67
Enabling, guidance activity, 26
English as a second language, 10
Equipment, 32, 33, 34, 41, 42, 43
    summary guidelines, 76
Evaluation, 68–9

Feeding back, guidance activity, 27–8
Finance for learning, 16–18
Firms, use of open learning, 9
Flexible learning, defined, 2
Further Education Unit, 19, 54

Giveaway literature, 41, 51
Gloucestershire County Library, 57, 59
Grants, 17
Guides, 39
Guiding, 65

Impartiality, 20, 23
Independent learning, defined, 2
Independent Library Learner Award, 5
Individual service to learners, 6
Industrial libraries, 32, 33, 34
Industry, training needs, 37
Information,
    about educational opportunities,
    19, 22, 42, 51
    about library services, 28–9
    related to advice, 20, 35

Information, *continued*
    statistics, 70
    training, 51-2
Information boards, 41
Information points, 32
Information skills,
    as library course, 16
    assessment, 25
    for learners, 15–6
Informing, guidance activity, 21–2
Inter-active video, 34, 39
Inventory slip, 48
Isolation, problem for learners, 10

Job centres, 36

Lead Body for Advice, Guidance and
    Counselling, 55
Learner, *see* Adult Independent
    Learner
Learning, place of libraries in, 1
Learning experience, 11–12
Learning materials policy, 5
Learning records, 11, 68
Library Association, 7, 29, 35
Library needs of learners, 11
Loan periods, 33, 48
Local education authorities, 36, 38
Local Enterprise Companies, 17, 44, 63
Local support networks, 4, 26, 31–2,
    34, 36–8, 43, 47, 54, 63
    statistics, 70
    summary guidelines, 75
Location of libraries, 30

Management games, 39
Marketing, 58–65
    summary guidelines, 76
    to parent body, 62–4
    to users, 60–2
Materials and Resources Information
    Service (MARIS), 37, 45
Mentor rôle, 48
Monitoring, 66–71
Multi-media stock, 5, 39–40

National Council for Educational
    Technology, 57

83

National Educational Guidance
  Initiative, 19, 29, 54, 55–6, 57
National Vocational Qualifications, 37
Networks, *see* Local support networks
Newspaper articles, 61

Open College, 10
Open College of the Arts, 10
Open learning, 2
  as entry to college courses, 11
Open Learning Federation, 37
Open Polytechnic, 10
Open University, 10, 36
Opening hours, 32, 33, 34

Performance monitoring, 66–71
Polytechnics, 36
Presentation of libraries, 64
Public libraries, 5, 20, 21, 29, 32, 33,
  34–5, 36
Public Libraries and Museums Act
  (1964), 5, 35
Publicity, 61–2

Quality control, 35–6

Reception facilities, 65
Retired people, 10

Sample frame of users, 67
Samples, 39
Second Chance Centre, Rhyl, 4
Second chance education group, 10
Self-employed people, 9
Service levels, 6, 32–6, 40–2, 69
  summary guidelines, 74–5
Signposting of libraries, 64
Single European Market, 9
Slides, 39
Small businesses, 9, 18
Staff, 31, 50–7
  advisory functions, 22–3
  approach to learners, 12
  summary guidelines, 76
Statistical records, 69–70
Stock, 28, 39–49
  evaluation, 68
  levels, 40–3

Stock, *continued*
  management, 48–9
  processing, 46
  selection, 43–6
  statistics, 70
  summary guidelines, 75–6
Study centres, 33–4, 42–3
Study courses, assessment, 13–14
Study facilities, 31, 34, 65, 70
Study planners, 39
Study records, 11, 68
Study skills, assessment, 14, 25

Targets for learning, 15
Townswomen's Guilds, 36
Trades unions, 37
Training, 34, 35, 38, 40, 50–9
  for educational guidance, 29
  schemes, 56–7
  statistics, 70
Training Access Points (TAPs), 22, 43,
  64
Training Agency, 55
Training and Enterprise Councils, 9,
  17, 36, 38, 44, 45, 55, 63
Training, Enterprise and Education
  Directorate (TEED), 7, 54
Tutor support, 33, 34, 43, 44, 47–8

Unemployed people, 18
Unit for the Development of Adult
  Continuing Education (UDACE),
  19, 54
Universities, 36
University of the Third Age, 36

Video tapes, 34, 39, 36
Vocational guidance, 24, 33
Voluntary agencies, 36

Welsh language, 10
Women returners, 9
Women's Institutes, 36
Workbooks, 33, 39
Workers' Educational Association, 36
Workplace education, 8, 17

Youth and community services, 36